THE COMPLETE GUIDE

PAINTING YOUR HOME

Doing it the Way a Professional Does, Inside and Out

JACK LUTS & PETE PETERSON

BETTERWAY PUBLICATIONS, INC.

WHITE HALL, VIRGINIA

Published by Betterway Publications, Inc.
Box 219
Crozet, VA 22932
(804) 823-5661

Cover by Susan Riley
Typography by East Coast Typography, Inc.

Library of Congress Cataloging-in-Publication Data

Luts, Jack
   The complete guide to painting your home : doing it the way a professional does, inside and out / Jack Luts & Pete Peterson.
      p.   cm.
   Includes index.
   ISBN: 1-55870-119-2 : $11.95
   1. House painting — Amateurs' manuals.   2. Interior decoration — Amateurs' manuals.   I. Peterson, Pete   II. Title.
TT320.L88   1989   88-37724
698'.1'028 — dc19   CIP

Printed in the United States of America
0 9 8 7 6 5 4 3 2

We dedicate this book to you —
the homeowner, do-it-yourself painter:

to making your next paint job look better and last longer;
to speeding up your work and making it easier;
to helping you have more fun while you're at it;
and to saving you money every time you pick up your brush.

Acknowledgments

Our thanks to:

Jim — Consultant, photo demonstrations
Sue and Kay — Typing
Marg and Kay — Illustrations
Mike — Computer-generated illustrations
Rick — Consultant
Photos and cover photo — Dean Michaels Studio
Illustrations — Jacob Rothmann

Contents

Introduction 9

1. About Paint 13

2. Preparation — Exterior 21

3. Exterior Prime Coat 25

4. Exterior Finish Coat 29

5. Interior Painting 37

6. Painting a Room with Wallpaper 57

7. About Wallcoverings 61

8. How to Hang Wallcoverings 65

9. Staining 79

10. Refinishing Floors 85

11. How to Figure a Job — Inside and Out 89

12. Care of Brushes, Paint, and Ladders 99

13. Equipment 107

14. Helpful Hints 117

15. Do It Yourself — with Others 127

16. The Way We Used to Do It 131

17. Most Common Mistakes 139

   Glossary 143

   Forms 147

   Index 157

Introduction

If your idea of painting is "first you borrow a ladder," this book is for you. Even if you have already painted half a dozen house exteriors and a baker's dozen interiors, you should still read it because there's a good chance that half of what you're doing is wrong . . . and as much as half of what you should be doing has not been a part of your past performances. Don't believe it? Read on and see if I'm not right.

There is a world of difference between covering a surface with paint and painting as a professional does. By the time you finish this book you'll know exactly how a professional does it. Knowing how doesn't automatically turn you into a professional painter, but with a little practice you'll easily sharpen your skills and save yourself a lot of time, effort, and money. The quality of your work will also improve greatly.

I am not conspiring to put your neighborhood painting contractor out of business. On the contrary, if your home needs painting and you can afford to have it done, I recommend that you do have it painted by a professional. There are at least two good reasons: it will be done without shortcuts, and it will be done in its entirety, within a short period of time. Many homeowners do half the job, then a sudden "crisis" somewhere else demands their time and part of the house goes unprotected for another winter.

In a very few paragraphs, I'll be getting into the actual work of painting, but first, allow me to present my credentials. J. Luts & Sons is a third generation painting firm in Madison, New Jersey, started in 1938 by my father, John Luts, Sr. Realizing that sons tend to know more than their fathers, my Dad arranged a three-year apprenticeship for me at another shop until I became a journeyman painter. Then he took me into his company as a full partner. By that time I still had a few things to learn, but I also knew that I had a pretty good teacher. Looking back, I realize that he was a fine craftsman as well as an excellent businessman. When my turn came, I made sure that my sons, Jim and Rick, learned the trade properly, and they are now running the company (assisted during the summer by my oldest son, Jack, an industrial arts teacher in the area).

We now do residential work primarily, but over the years we have done all kinds of painting and decorating including the beautiful Hartley Dodge Memorial Building (our town hall) and most of the churches in Madison at least once, both inside and out.

Madison is next door to Morristown, New Jersey,

where George Washington and his Continental Army spent the winter of 1777 and endured the "terrible winter" of 1779-80. We're just a handful of miles from Fort Nonsense and from Jockey Hollow, where the Wicke House still stands. (If you're a Revolutionary War history buff, you know that a young lady named Tempe Wicke hid her horse in this house to prevent it being stolen by a small band of mutineering Pennsylvania Line soldiers . . . or so the story goes.)

In our part of the country, an old house is pre-Revolution and it's surprising how many of these homes are still in use; most of them remarkably well preserved by the loving care of the owners . . . and good paint.

Madison is considered by many to be a "bedroom" community of New York City because a good percentage of our work force commutes the twenty-five miles into the city. More than a few of our customers are "board level" executives. It's been a common practice over the years for a number of our regular customers to hand us their keys when they take off for their winter vacations and expect to find their rooms redecorated on their return. Not to brag — just to make the point that J. Luts & Sons has worked for some very particular cus-

Some years ago we bought and rehabilitated two old residences on Elmer Street in Madison, and converted them to retail business use. Luts Paint Center uses the first floor and basement.

tomers. We've had these families with us for three generations. Still do.

The fact that I've spent a lifetime as a practicing professional painter doesn't necessarily qualify me to write a book on the subject. But our paint store does. And that's the reason for this book. Each day that we're open, I give away a free painting lesson with just about every can of paint we sell.

It's the one-on-one conversations with our customers that have convinced me the average home-owner who comes in our shop really would like to know how to do it himself or herself. And do it

right! These are people from all walks of life. And except for the people who come into our shop, they probably have nowhere else to find out and no one to ask.

So the purpose of this book is to tell you — just as if you were standing across the counter at Luts' Paint Center, 4 Elmer Street, and wondering what kind of paint to use or how you should handle a specific painting problem. I've tried to answer everything you've ever wanted to know. And lots more you never thought of. I'll go through it a step at a time, from start to finish. First outside, then inside, and top to bottom.

Coauthor Jack Luts tinting color in a gallon of latex enamel paint. A little color goes a long way. The formula for each customer's color is written on the can for future use.

1
About Paint

EXTERIOR PAINT

When you are considering painting the exterior of your house, the purchase of your paint is the first step in an action that involves considerable time and money, as well as the appearance of your home for the next five to six years. Buying the paint in itself frightens off many homeowners from ever attempting the job. (A visit to the paint department of any large discount store will remind you how confusing it can be.)

This book is intended to be a reference manual as well as a how-to-do-it instruction guide. We want to explain the "why" as well as the "how." We will provide you with an easy guide for choosing the right paint for your needs, but first you should know something about the paints you will choose from. Your paint dealer can be of great help in making the right decision, but if you are dealing with a part-time clerk in the paint department of a discount store, you may very well know more than he or she does, especially after reading this chapter.

What is Exterior Paint?

The standard oil base exterior house paint is a mixture of pigment and vehicle. The pigment is ground up solids which will probably be listed as titanium and calcium carbonate and perhaps others on the label. The vehicle will be listed as either linseed oil or alkyd, plus driers. A latex paint will differ in that the vehicle is water instead of oil.

When either oil paint or latex paint is applied to a surface, exposure to oxygen changes the liquid to a hard dry coat which offers long-lasting protection against weather and provides a decorative appearance as well.

The one important thing to remember with any paint is "you gotta stir it." The pigments are suspended which means they'll settle. Always stir well before using. And have it shaken when you buy it.

There are then, two basic paints used for house painting: water base and oil base, and these are labeled as follows.

- Water Base paints are called LATEX. The word "acrylic" sometimes precedes "latex" on the label. Acrylic means that a plastic resin has been added. Latex paints come in a flat, mid-gloss, or high-gloss finish. (You can buy different specialty paints such as trim paint, floor paint, etc., but our concern here is exterior house paint.)

■ Oil Base paints come in two types: the standard exterior paint, usually made with linseed oil, and an ALKYD, a synthetic oil paint that has been rapidly gaining in popularity since World War II.

We have found that alkyd paints perform just as well as linseed oil paints; in fact, they have a couple of advantages over the traditional paints. Alkyd sets up and dries faster and, most important, alkyd is the paint you are likely to find in the paint department of your discount store. Linseed oil paints will be carried by all paint stores because they are often preferred by professional painters who feel that linseed oil is easier to work with than alkyd. On a personal note, we are firm believers in oil base primers, even when we plan to use a latex finish paint.

Latex finish paints have several important advantages. They have a better color retention than oil paints; they hold their color better and longer, especially in the very deep colors. They dry fast and can be safely used over a damp surface. In addition, some latex primers have been formulated to stop cedar or redwood bleed. (The tannic acids in these woods sometimes bleed thorough oil-based paints.) Another advantage is the absence of odors, which is very desirable for indoor work. For many people, the biggest advantage of all is the fact that latex cleans up more easily than oil base paints. (Just use soap and water.)

Some disadvantages are: latex primers must be applied liberally; you shouldn't apply a latex paint at temperatures below fifty degrees or in the direct, hot summer sun; it can be washed off by a sudden shower if the coat hasn't had a chance to set up. And, this might be personal or perhaps it's the brushes we use, but we've noticed that latex paint is harder to cut in around a window sash or for any kind of fine work.

Both latex and oil paints come in primer and finish labels. I am assuming that your house exterior will need two coats. Most houses do. The word "prim-er" refers to the outside first coat of paint. (The first coat of interior woodwork is called "undercoat.")

Many homeowners don't use a primer at all but instead buy a finish paint and give the surface two coats of that. The label may say that you can do this — the phrase "self-covering" is often used. It's okay to do this if the first coat is a flat paint. A second coat of glossy finish over a first coat of glossy finish could cause your paint to chip and peel. Your best bet is to use a flat primer for the first coat. It's formulated to provide a good base for the finish paint.

What Paint Should You Buy?

These are your options:

■ You can use a latex or an oil base primer. It should be a flat finish.

■ You can use a latex or an oil base finish paint. Either flat or glossy.

Whichever you decide, make sure that your primer will dry flat to hold a finish, whether it's latex or oil.

To simplify your decision, we recommend this procedure.

☐ Use an oil base flat primer. We have found in most instances that an oil base primer is the safest all-around primer to use.

☐ Use an oil finish — if you are painting your house white.

☐ Use a latex finish — if you are using a color. It has a better color retention.

☐ Use a gloss or mid-gloss finish — if your siding is new or relatively new. It looks nicer.

☐ Use a flat finish — if your siding is old or rough. It will hide imperfections better.

Most major manufacturers can offer just about any color you want in either oil or latex finish paints. Paint stores and paint departments usually carry a complete line of (depending on the company) anywhere from twelve to twenty-four standard colors. You can also choose from a color chart or have any of hundreds of shades and tints custom mixed to a formula and blended by machine. Custom mixes can vary somewhat, so it is advisable to order all of your color finish paint at one time so that you can mix them together to get one uniform color. Even standard colors vary from batch to batch.

Primer paints usually come in white. If you intend to finish in white, leave the primer as is. If you are using a color finish, have the dealer tint your primer toward the color you intend to use. Use a deep gray primer for a red or black finish.

IMPORTANT: Make sure the paint store shakes your paint.

What Brand Should You Buy?

This is a good rule to follow: Don't try to save money on paint. Buy a top-of-the-line product made by a major manufacturer who has been in business for a while. You can find the familiar names by looking in your Yellow Pages under "Paint — Retail."

When you consider the number of hours and amount of effort it takes to paint your house, the dollar difference between an unknown brand "on sale" and a major, nationally advertised brand is petty cash. Don't risk it! You want your paint job to look good and you want that protection to last. You don't want to do it again in a hurry.

As a professional painter who owns and operates a paint store, I naturally lean in that direction when it comes to buying paint. We won't carry an inferior product and we won't mislead a customer to make a sale. We're sure most paint store dealers feel the way we do. We know our products and can

offer advice when a customer needs help. Most paint stores do.

Another important consideration when deciding whether to use an oil base or a water base paint pertains to the cleanup of your brushes. This is of special importance to apartment dwellers, particularly when painting interiors. After using an oil base paint, the brush should be cleaned with mineral spirits or paint thinner; brushes used in water base paint are cleaned with warm water and soap. The proper technique for cleaning brushes is fully covered in Chapter 14: Helpful Hints.

INTERIOR PAINT

Walls and Ceilings

I know it's confusing to walk past the rows of paint in a mass marketing outlet, but it will be much easier to make a purchase when you know what you're looking for. To paint a room in your home, you'll probably need two kinds of paint: Wall & Ceiling Paint and Trim, or Woodwork Paint. Let's discuss them one at a time.

You have the option of using oil base paint, but most wall and ceiling paint used today — by homeowners and professional painters alike — is latex or water base paint. There are at least three major advantages.

1. Latex has very little odor. (Oil paint has a strong odor.)

2. It's easy to clean up. (Soap and water vs. paint thinner or mineral spirits.)

3. It dries fast. (About two hours vs. overnight for oil paint.)

To a painter, this is very important. It means that he can cover the ceiling and walls and then apply the finish coat the same day, without having to allow a day between for the paint to dry, as he would if he were using an oil base paint. He would also have to close off the room overnight to make

You can open a paint can with a stiff knife or a screwdriver, but a paint can opener is best. (Your dealer has them.) Make sure a dropcloth is under the can.

It's a good idea to remove the paint from your stick after stirring the paint. Why waste paint?

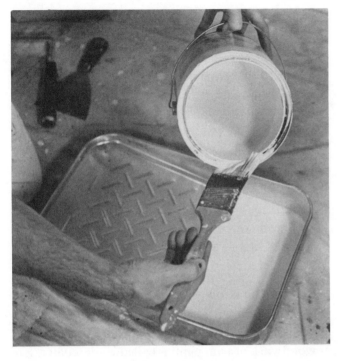

After you pour paint in the roller tray, wipe the rim of the paint can with your brush so that paint doesn't run down the side of the label.

This is the first step in cleaning a roller. "Milk" off the paint with the dull side of a knife . . . even a kitchen knife . . . to squeeze out most of the paint. You'll be amazed at how much paint a roller holds. Then wash it with clear water, if you're using latex paint.

certain that someone or some pet didn't brush up against the walls and smear the paint.

So many improvements in wall and ceiling paint have been made in recent years that many painters feel a good latex paint is as good as oil in almost every category; it lasts as long, stands up under cleaning, and certainly looks every bit as good as oil. There are special circumstances where an oil base paint is essential, but we'll cover those later. Meantime, let's concentrate on latex wall and ceiling paint. There are two types, for two specific purposes: Latex Primer & Sealer (for walls and ceiling) and Ceiling Flat Finish. We would use both and recommend that you do also.

Many homeowners — encouraged by paint manufacturer advertising — will try to get away with the application of one coat. Then, if it does need a second coat, they will use the same paint for the finish coat. And that's perfectly okay. A Flat Finish Wall and Ceiling Paint is designed to be self-covering.

We don't follow that practice because a Primer & Sealer coat first, followed by a Flat Finish paint, will probably do a better job. If you plan to use both Primer & Sealer and Flat Finish paints, buy them at the same time and have the Primer & Sealer tinted to nearly the same shade as your finish coat.

The Flat Finish coat, as mentioned earlier, can be applied about two hours after the Primer & Sealer application. Use the fingernail test to make sure the primer is dry. Simply scratch the painted surface with your fingernail. If the paint comes off under your nail, it's not dry enough.

Trim Paint

You should not use Wall & Ceiling paint on woodwork; for this you need Enamel Undercoater (or just Undercoater) and Enamel Finish. Each comes in latex and oil forms.

Undercoater is a flat paint that has been formulated to stick on existing paint and to provide a bond for your finish coat. We suggest that you use a Latex Enamel Undercoater (in preference to oil) for all the reasons listed previously; namely, it's easier. Whereas you can apply two finish coats of Wall & Ceiling Paint, one over the other, the manufacturer usually doesn't recommend that you do this with Enamel Finish Paint, especially if it's a glossy finish. If you do, there's a good chance it will chip off in a shorter time than otherwise. Again, you need undercoater and finish. However, wash surfaces first to assure a good bond, before applying undercoater.

So that you know what to look for, the terminology is as follows: The first coat of wall and ceiling paint is called Primer/Sealer. The first coat of woodwork or trim paint is called Undercoater. No big deal, but that's the way the label will read.

Both oil and latex enamel finish paints have varying degrees of shine ranging from satin sheen, semi-gloss to high gloss. The last is seldom used on walls but can be applied to outdoor furniture and possibly kitchen trim. The most popular variety is semi-gloss or satin. We suggest that here also, you use a Latex Finish paint for all the previously listed reasons.

I must confess that we prefer an oil base enamel finish paint because the paint seems to flow out better without leaving any streaks or brush marks, and we feel that it lasts longer. Some latex paints have a tendency to stick slightly in warm, humid weather, which could be a problem with windows. Also bookshelves and table tops may become sticky, especially when you put something of any weight on a latex painted surface. However, this might be our own idiosyncrasy, and the ease of cleaning up certainly gives the advantage to latex for the casual painter.

INTERIOR HOUSE
Simplified Paint Purchase Guide

Latex Primer & Sealer — Comes in white, can be tinted and used on ceiling and walls as first coat.

Latex Wall & Ceiling Finish — Should be tinted to your color. This is a flat paint that is self-covering.

Latex Undercoater/Sealer Trim — This is a flat paint for woodwork. Comes in white, can be tinted.

Latex Enamel Semi-Gloss (or Satin Finish) — For woodwork. This should be tinted to your color, or select a ready-made shade.

All Paints Are Not Created Equal

The basic difference between exterior and interior paint is that the pigment is ground more finely for the inside paint and exterior paint has more elasticity, especially the oil base paints. The major benefit of interior paint is to provide an attractive cover that also protects.

Not too many years ago there was a rule which held that you should never use an exterior paint for indoor use, especially if it were an oil base paint. Today, there are latex paints that are perfectly safe and effective, indoors and out. The manufacturer will clearly state that fact if it is a "one-size-fits-all" paint.

As a professional painter, I would still hesitate to use an oil base exterior paint indoors. The results certainly wouldn't be catastrophic if I did, but it would take a lot longer to dry and the color would darken faster than if I had used a paint especially formulated for indoor work. There would also be an odor.

You might be guided by this common sense rule of thumb. Painting is a time-consuming occupation for the average homeowner. At the very least, it's at the expense of something else you could be doing (like golfing, fishing, or even taking a nap). That being so, you want the finished job to last so you don't have to repeat the work in a hurry. By using a good brand of the proper paint and following the step-by-step procedures outlined in this book, you'll be able to do a good, professional-looking job that will last a long time. You'll also give your home the protection it needs and the attractive look you want. In short, it's worthwhile to do it right.

ABOUT LABELS

Buying paint is often confusing. A knowledgeable paint dealer can be valuable in helping you to select what you need to do the job you intend to accomplish. However, if you are on your own as you examine the shelves of paint cans, you would not be alone if you were somewhat confused about which paint is best for your specific task.

Each paint manufacturer uses his own nomenclature in labeling his line of paints. His front label is designed to make it as attractive as possible for you to buy his brand of paint rather than his competitor's. We have generally stayed away from recommending brand names, and our generic description of the kind of paint to buy for a specific job might, at times, be at variance with the label that you'll see on your paint supplier's shelves.

For example, in Chapter 5: Interior Painting, we specify using a Latex Primer and a Wall & Ceiling Finish Paint. At most paint stores you'll be able to find these. But some manufacturers sell separate wall and ceiling paints.

The paint company is selling ceiling paint (often labeled Ceiling White) separately, because many homeowners want a white ceiling. And he's selling "One Coat" because every other paint company is.

Most homeowners want tinted wall covering. So he's selling that separately — again, "One Coat."

In short, if you want your ceiling white, you can buy his Flat Ceiling White paint. Use one or two coats of this paint, depending on how it looks. (The basic fact remains — two is better.) And you can buy his tinted Flat Wall Paint and apply one coat or two, as above. If you want your ceiling the same color as the walls, buy a wall paint and use it for the ceiling as well.

However, the manufacturer's marketing approach — selling separate wall and ceiling paints — makes sense from his point of view. Most labels, as you will note, stress ONE COAT. Again, the manufacturer is selling paint; we're not. We're explaining the right way to do the job for the best appearance and the longest lasting results. If you take shortcuts that's okay, but at least you'll know the proper way, whether you decide to follow the instructions or not.

SUMMARY

Exterior

■ Two basic exterior paints: latex (water base) and alkyd (oil base). Both come in primer and finish labels.

■ Most houses need two coats.

■ Purchase options: 1) Use a latex or oil base primer — but only flat. 2) Use a latex or oil base finish — either flat or glossy.

We are firm believers in using oil base primers even with a latex finish coat. Whichever you use, make sure the paint store machine shakes the paint.

Interior

■ Advantages of latex paint: little odor, easy to clean (soap and water vs. paint thinner for oil base paints), dries fast.

■ Two coats — primer and finish — look better than just finish coat on walls and ceilings.

■ Don't use wall & ceiling paint on woodwork. Use enamel undercoater and enamel finish.

■ Don't try to save money on paint; buy a name brand. Good paint will help your paint job look good and last long.

■ Buying paint can be confusing. Ask the dealer for advice but know in advance what you want.

2
Preparation — Exterior

EQUIPMENT NEEDED

☐ Extension ladder and/or stepladder

☐ Chisel knife and hook scraper

☐ Sandpaper (coarse)

☐ Scrub brush (bristle type that can screw on a mop handle or extension pole)

☐ Rubber gloves

☐ Duster or cloth

☐ Garden hose

☐ Liquid bleach (such as Clorox)

☐ Powdered detergent (such as Spic and Span or Soilex)

☐ W-D 40 or other silicone spray

☐ Goggles (type that fits over glasses if you wear them)

Preparation is the nasty part of the job. But it's probably the most important part because it will add to, or subtract from, the number of years the finished surface will last. Unfortunately, it's Step One, and after it's completed your house might look worse than before you started. However, it will be clean and that's "condition one."

Don't shortcut either of the two essential parts of the preparation process: washing and scraping. How well you handle these tasks can make or break the entire job.

Before you get started, when the siding is dry, you might run your hand along its surface. There's a good chance that your hand will be covered with a chalky dust. If so, that's good. It's the paint wearing away the way it should, rather than building up. But it's also one of the reasons for painting — too much could have worn away. The chalk should be washed off, along with the dirt and dust that have accumulated. The result after your preparation should be a good, clean, hard, and dry surface that will allow paint to bond.

MILDEW REMOVAL

The exterior surfaces to be painted should be washed to kill any mildew, get rid of the chalky paint on the siding, and to clean off the accumulation of dust and road dirt. You can accomplish all of this in one operation. It's a good idea to finish washing all sides of the house before starting to scrape.

Almost all houses have mildew. It's most prevalent on the shady side of the house, especially behind bushes or shrubs, and it thrives on dampness, shade, and heat. Mildews and molds are both classes of fungi. The names are often used interchangeably. Actually, mold is a saprophyte, or feeder on dead material, and mildew is a parasite, or feeder on living things.

We use the word mildew to describe the condition that looks like a black discoloration on the side of the house. It's really a network of white spores covered with a black powder. Unless they are killed, the mildew spores will keep spreading. If you paint over the mildew it will still come through, and in time even push the paint off the wood. However, don't be surprised if the mildew keeps coming back, year after year.

We kill and remove mildew with a solution of three parts water and one part Clorox (or any bleach) to which is added a half cup of detergent. For example, three quarts of water to one quart of bleach, plus ½ cup of detergent. (Soilex works well for us.) Don't make your bucket too full, especially if you have to climb a ladder.

WARNING: Use caution when applying this solution with either a sponge or a bristle brush. Wear goggles to protect your eyes and a hat. Also wear rubber gloves on your hands and don't let the solution trickle down onto the exposed skin of your wrist and arm, which can easily happen when you are working on overheads such as a porch ceiling. The condition of a sleeve or glove cuff rubbing against your bare wrist, if it is wet with cleaning solution trickling down your hand, could cause a severe chemical burn.

If you spill any solution on bare skin, make sure you rinse well with cold water, and consult the instructions and precautions on the label. Splashes and spilled solution on clothes could remove the color, so wear old clothes for the job. And don't work in a strong wind.

Using a mop handle on your scrub brush will make it easier to reach all of the mildew infestations. You should also use reasonable caution to keep the solution from dripping on shrubs and plants. (We usually hose down shrubs later with fresh water.)

WARNING: Use extreme caution when handling a ladder around electrical wires. Assume every wire is live. An aluminum ladder can be dangerous if it is damp with dew or wet from your hose.

To continue your mildew removal, start at the top and work down, going over the entire side of your house including the window sills. After you've finished, the bleach/detergent solution must be washed off, which you can easily do with a gentle spray of your garden hose. Spraying with a pressure nozzle can easily break a window. (If you do inadvertently spray the glass, it would be a nice gesture to complete the task of washing the windows.)

Complete the mildew removal and fresh water rinse operation on each side of your house, then quit for the day while you wait for the wood to dry. Since most people (usually men) like to splash water, this part of the job is not that tedious. Scraping is the chore. You might do yourself a favor here. After you finish scraping one side, you might encourage yourself by getting out the paintbrush and applying the primer on that side before getting back to scraping the rest of the house. It's a nice change of pace and a lot more fun.

THE SCRAPING JOB

At this point, you're looking for loose paint. This can be removed with a scraper or chisel knife. If possible, always scrape with the grain of the wood. When you make a vertical mark on a horizontal grain the scratch will always show up, even though it's covered with two coats of paint.

Use a file to sharpen one side of your scraper and/or chisel knife from time to time. You don't need it sharp enough to shave with, but it will do its job better if it's reasonably sharp. A razor blade that slides in and out of a safety holder is the best tool to scrape the dried paint from window glass.

You can also use a belt or vibrating power sander for scraping. (Circular sanders leave swirls on the wood.) Remove the loose paint only. Leave the tight cracked paint alone because it will provide a good enough surface for your primer. Besides, you probably couldn't get it off anyway unless you burned it off. But do make sure that you clean off the dust or residue from scraping. We use a duster brush, but an old paintbrush or a cloth will also work.

Paint can be removed by burning with a propane torch. This method removes all of the old paint down to the wood, so you can start off as if it were raw wood. It is now seldom used on an entire house because of the cost, but it is sometimes used on window and door sills and small areas. Paint deteriorates more rapidly on flat horizontal surfaces which hold water. If the condition of your house is such that the paint must be torched off, hire a professional — it's tricky and dangerous. More than that, your insurance company probably wouldn't want you to tackle it yourself. (In some states it's illegal to remove paint with a torch.)

After you've washed and scraped, you should find that most of the surface is hard and clean. However, you will see places that need "tightening" up; places that need putty, caulking, or maybe even wood filler. But don't do this yet. It's best to wait until after the prime coat has been applied. Otherwise the oils in the caulking and putty will be absorbed by the wood. This will cause them to dry up and shrink, and ultimately to fall out, allowing moisture to seep in.

This last note, incidentally, expresses the theme and purpose of this book. Do it right and you'll have to do it less often. Your finished job will look better longer, you will protect your investment better, and you'll save time and money along the way.

One final plea for proper preparation before you put on the primer. Some years ago (before we opened our paint store), a man called us for help less than a year after he had painted his entire house. He hadn't bothered to prepare it. He thought that all he had to do was to apply the new paint over the old, which was very chalky, for starters. He completely ignored chalk and gloss and not only wasted the cost of the paint and a good part of his summer painting, but he had to start over from scratch and then repaint.

COMMON QUESTIONS ABOUT EXTERIOR PAINTING

Q. *How long should house paint last?*

A. Two coats of a quality paint, correctly applied to a properly prepared surface, should last at least five and, in some cases, as many as eight to ten years.

Q. *What is the best time of year for painting?*

A. Any time of year is okay provided the temperature does not drop below fifty degrees Fahrenheit (or whatever temperature the manufacturer specifies on the paint can). Do not paint in conditions of extreme heat. Never paint a surface in direct sunlight.

Q. *Should I use a house paint with a gloss or flat finish?*

A. A gloss finish is smoother and easier to clean. A flat finish minimizes irregularities in the exterior surface. Most people prefer a flat finish for the siding of the house and gloss for trim, windows, and doors.

Q. *Can I paint over aluminum siding?*

A. Yes. Be sure to purchase an exterior paint recommended for use on aluminum siding or ask the salesperson in the paint store for advice.

Q. *What is the best way to apply exterior paint?*

A. A 4″ brush is best for applying flat or gloss paint to clapboard or lap siding. A roller can be used with flat paint on large even surfaces.

Q. *Isn't one heavy coat of paint as good as two normal coats?*

A. No. The paint won't cure properly and will probably peel and crack much sooner than two coats.

Q. *What causes house paint to blister or peel?*

A. The two most common causes are not preparing the surface properly and the presence of moisture in the surface.

Q. *Are all exterior surfaces paintable?*

A. Yes, with a few exceptions such as slate roofs and glazed tile.

SUMMARY

■ Wash house exterior with solution of bleach and detergent. Wear rubber gloves and goggles.

■ Use a scrub brush or sponge to apply; this will kill mildew and remove dirt.

■ Hose down side of house with fresh water.

■ When dry, scrape or sand loose paint and dust off residue.

■ Use extreme caution when moving your ladder around electrical wires, especially when working with water.

3
Exterior
Prime Coat

EQUIPMENT NEEDED

☐ Duster

☐ Brushes (three brush kit)

☐ Dropcloths

☐ Clean cloth (for wiping)

☐ Scrapers

☐ Rope and pegs

☐ Shrubbery clippers

☐ Pothook (for hooking paint bucket to ladder rung)

The two basic reasons for painting are preservation and cosmetics, with preservation being by far the most important. By the time your house has begun to look a bit shabby, the paint has probably lost much of its protective qualities.

Unless stated otherwise, all of our painting instructions pertain to wood surfaces; we will discuss other surfaces such as concrete, aluminum siding, etc., separately in Chapter 4.

MEASURING YOUR HOUSE EXTERIOR

Before you rush out to buy your primer paint, let's find out exactly how much you'll need. A professional painter can come within a gallon of the right amount just by looking over your house — carefully. However, he's using a basic formula to come up with the total number of gallons he expects to use.

Here are two ways to do it: first, the shorthand version, then the exact way to measure.

To estimate the number of gallons needed to paint the outside of a house, simply allow one gallon for every room in the house. Count hallways as rooms, and make allowances for the exterior condition of the house. Thus, a six room frame house with an upper and a lower hall would require approximately eight gallons of prime coat and approximately seven gallons for the finish coat. (The finish coat on primed surfaces usually spreads more easily and goes further.)

The most accurate way to determine the amount of paint needed is to measure the number of square feet on each side of the house. To do this, multiply the length times the height in feet for each side.

Measure along the ground with a tape measure if

you have one, or pace off the distance if you don't. As every football fan knows, one good step equals three feet. Measure the height from the ground up to the roof line only. Figure the gable by measuring the height from the base of the triangle to the peak of the roof. The base is the same as your length along the ground, of course. Multiply the height from the base by the length, and divide by two. (The gable is that triangular part of the wall under a pitched roof from the cornice — the roof line over the gutters — to the peak, which is the top part of the roof.)

You might not be able to get a tape measure from the cornice to the peak, so you can accurately estimate the gable height this way. Measure one of the clapboards at ground level; they usually have a 4" or 6" reveal (the part showing). Then count the number of boards and divide by two (if a 6" reveal) or by three (if a 4" reveal), and you'll have the height in feet. You can also measure a shingle (usually they have a 6" or 10" reveal), and count the rows. Then divide by two (if a 6" reveal), or simply call each row one foot if it has a 10" reveal.

Side: 30′ L × 10′ H = 300 sq. ft.

Gable: 30′ (along base of triangle) × 10′ H = 300 sq. ft. divided by 2 = 150 sq. ft.

Total side: 450 sq. ft. One side.

Then add up the totals for each side and you have the total area in square feet. Measure each side separately because each could be different. Using the example above, a typical one family, two story house might average 1500 square feet. Ignore the windows when you are measuring. True, the window trim will not use as much paint as a solid surface, but this will allow you room for error.

The label on every one gallon can of paint will tell you the number of square feet that particular paint will cover under ordinary conditions. Divide that number (say 350 square feet) into your total square footage for all sides, and you have the number of gallons you need for the entire house.

GET READY

It's important when you buy finish paint, and usually a pretty good idea when you pick up your primer paint, to purchase enough to finish the entire job. You probably know what your finish color will be, so you should have your paint store tint your primer, which usually comes in white. If your finish color is white, don't tint the primer; you'll have no problem painting white finish on your flat white primer. Just make sure that your primer isn't tinted substantially darker or lighter than your finish coat. And don't select a primer tint that will be hard to live with if something unforeseen should happen and your finish coat cannot be applied for some time. (We have a neighbor whose barn-red garage wore a shocking pink front for the entire winter when cold weather came unseasonably early last winter.)

Our current practice in deciding whether to use latex or oil base paint (as described in Chapter 1) is this:

■ If the house is to be painted white, use oil base primer and finish. (If you don't mind using oil.)

■ If the house is to be a color, use an oil base primer and a latex finish.

Professional painters usually use lightweight canvas dropcloths when painting exteriors; probably most homeowners will not. However, they are worth the investment because they're long lasting and they will protect your shrubs, walks, roofs, and anything directly under wherever you're painting. Plastic dropcloths cost less and do offer protection, but there are a couple of cautions. They can kill shrubs on a hot day and they are slippery on roofs and floors. A better option might be a throwaway paper dropcloth which is both effective and inexpensive.

Shrubs should be trimmed back to allow you to work behind them, or at least tied back to a tree or a peg driven into the ground. (We carry pegs and ropes for just that purpose.) When you cover flowers with a dropcloth, place stakes in the ground about two feet apart, so the plants won't be crushed by the weight. Where there are low plants that might be stepped on, we use a couple of step-ladders and put a plank between them so that we can work from the plank, rather than risk crushing a customer's prize "whatevers."

We'll discuss brushes in more detail later, but you should have a painter's kit of three standard brushes. These consist of: a 1½" or 2" brush for fine work such as windows, spindles, etc.; a 3" brush for doors and window frames; and a 4" brush for the siding, or body of the house. You can paint any given surface with these three.

GET SET

This observation might seem petty, but there is a right way to dip a brush so the paint doesn't stream all over. It also involves the use of a proper container. As you know, most house paint comes in gallon containers. These are too full to work with (or to stir), so don't try. Find or buy an empty gallon can, plastic pail, or bucket with a handle. (You can use an old, empty gallon paint can. It can be any color. Your new paint won't mix with the old, provided it's dry and hardened.) This container should be your "work bucket." After your paint is well stirred (it will have settled after being machine-shaken at the paint store), pour off about a quart into your work bucket. You now have room enough to dip your brush about an inch deep into the paint. Keeping the brush within the bucket, tap the brush in the front and again in the back of the bucket to knock off the excess paint and keep it from dripping. Don't drag the brush across the top of the can because you'll skimp on the amount of paint applied to your surface.

If you have to thin the paint, do it in your work bucket only, because if you over-thin it, you'll still have the heavier paint in the original can to bring it back again. Wipe off the edge of the original can after pouring to prevent the paint from slopping

down the side. Neatness counts. How else could painters wear whites?

GO!

You're finally ready to paint — if you have your equipment in place and your brush handy. Since you should start from the top and work down, your ladder should be securely placed against the side of the house. Never reach out too far to either side while working from a ladder. A good safety measure is to crook one arm around the sidepiece. This will prevent you from reaching out too far on the opposite side. (See Chapter 13: Equipment.)

After painting one section, climb down and move the ladder over, then work down to the approximate level you have finished and move again. To make ladder handling as easy as possible, we start at one side and when we reach the other end we lower the ladder and work our way back.

Never place your ladder on an area that you have just painted. It not only spoils your nice paint job, it's also slippery and dangerous. Keep your ladder under the area you're painting. Don't paint over other people working below. Even if you don't drop a tool on them, you could spatter paint.

When applying paint, lay it off with the grain of the wood, which is usually horizontal. (Wood shingles should be laid off vertically.)

Weather is an important factor in painting exteriors. The house must be completely dry when using an oil base paint. More than that, you should have a full day of dry weather preceding because water collects in cracks and crevices, and even though the house seems dry, the areas under porches and overhangs could be damp. Painting over any of these wet areas could cause trouble spots before you start. It's also interesting to note that the wind will dry off a house quicker than the sun. Whenever possible, do the exposed part of the house first. Save the sheltered porch, where you can also paint the screens and shutters, for a rainy day.

Dampness is not as critical a factor with latex paint. In fact, it's okay to paint over dampness (not wetness) . . . let's say a couple of hours after a shower . . . but you must be careful that the rain doesn't start up again and hit your paint before it has a chance to set up. If it does, the rain could wash off the latex paint or streak it down the side of the house. However, you should be aware of the temperature when using latex paint. Except for the summer months, it's generally wise to knock off in mid-afternoon. Temperatures usually drop as the sun goes down, and the cool, damp air can cause the paint to streak before it has a chance to set. It's also a good idea to read the label carefully, and refer to it from time to time, especially as conditions change. If the paint manufacturer says not to paint at temperatures lower than fifty degrees . . . believe him.

SUMMARY

■ Measure the painting surface of the house for each side.

■ Determine how much paint you need.

■ Unless you are using a white finish, have the paint store tint your primer. Oil base primer is preferable.

■ Use dropcloths for the work area; protect plants and shrubs.

■ Make sure your painting surface is completely dry — this is critical with oil base primer, less so with latex.

■ Don't paint when the temperature drops (read label to check critical temperature).

4
Exterior Finish Coat

The finish coat is the rewarding part of house painting. The real reason that most homeowners paint is to make their houses look nice again, and the finish coat does that from the very first stroke. Everything about it is better than primer: the paint is slicker, it spreads more easily, and the dried coat gleams in the sunlight, especially if you're using a glossy finish. The payoff comes when your neighbors say, "Hey, your house looks great." It's also comforting to know that you won't have to do it again for about six years or more. If you do it right.

The procedural steps are almost the same as painting your prime coat, but there are some differences. You'll be using a different paint, of course, and perhaps different brushes (bristle for oil base paint, nylon or polyester for latex). You will also be applying a second finish paint if you're using a contrasting trim. And you should carry (or have handy) putty to fill the holes and caulking to fill the cracks that you have painted over with primer.

The same basic rules apply: paint from the top down, complete one side at a time, and follow the instructions on the label. But before you start, "box" the paint, if you are using a color.

All of your one gallon cans of finish paint should have been recently machine shaken. Open them (not more than four) and pour the paint into a clean empty five gallon can, making certain that there's no pigment residue left at the bottom of any of the one gallon cans. Stir the five gallon can thoroughly. You box the paint to make sure that the entire house will be one shade. Even factory-mixed cans of the same color can vary from one batch to the next. (If you can't box your paint, just make sure that you don't change cans in the middle of a side.) After you have poured out an amount of paint into your work bucket, make sure that you seal the five gallon can tightly so a skin won't develop on the surface.

As you work, if you should ever want to thin out your paint, make sure that you only do this in your work bucket. You'll need your heavy paint in the five gallon can to thicken the paint if you over-thin it. (Use thinner or mineral spirits for oil base paint and water for latex.) At the end of the day, pour anything left over in your work bucket back into the five gallon can. Wipe your work bucket clean with your brush, pouring into your five gallon can. The residue in the work bucket will dry overnight, and the next day you can pour fresh paint on top of this.

NOTE: Oil base paint will develop a skin on top if left for any length of time. To help prevent this, sprinkle a very small amount of thinner over the surface of the paint. You can do this by dipping a clean brush in the thinner and shaking it over the paint. Place a sheet of plastic wrap over the top of the can before putting on the lid. Then hammer the lid firmly closed. If a skin does form, run a knife around the container and lift out the skin in one piece. If it breaks, strain the paint through a wire strainer. While latex paint is less likely to form a skin than oil paint, it will develop if the lid is left off overnight, or sometimes when working directly in the hot sun.

TRIM

One of the things that differentiates a professional painting job from that of the average homeowner, even to the casual observer, is the way the painter handles the trim. A professional paints everything: the window sills and sashes, the foundation, doors, the mailbox, outdoor lights, fences, garage door handles or hinges, lattice work, iron railings, and shutters. Trim, then, is everything that isn't roof, siding, window glass, or blockwork (the founda-

tion). Trim is like a frame for a portrait or the accessories on a well-dressed woman. It sets off the beauty of your home. Don't shortchange yourself by ignoring this work. Since painting trim can pose some special problems, we will treat each part individually.

Windows

If you are painting a color on the siding, you might want to paint the windows the same color as the rest of the house. If you're using white, you might use a black or contrasting color trim. In this event, it's important to remember that trim paint is specially formulated to make it non-chalking so that the color doesn't bleed onto the white siding. It's especially important to use non-chalking paint if you are painting the windows on a natural brick or stone house.

If you are painting the house and trim the same color, and your paint is non-chalking as a good latex will be, then all you have to do is switch brushes and continue painting when you get to the windows. You may want to try to do this especially if you have second story windows that must be reached by a ladder. Paint the trim while you're up there.

A professional painter will carry both pots of paint (on separate pothooks) and both brushes. He will be skilled enough to paint wet to wet, i.e., lay the black trim alongside the white siding paint without having one run into the other. He's able to save time and energy by not having to climb up and down the ladder or having to wait until the siding paint sets before doing the trim.

The best approach for a homeowner, however, is to paint the windows separately, either before or after the siding. If you do the windows first, you'll have no problems with scratching the newly painted siding finish. Most people prefer to do them last because they're anxious to get the siding covered and a six-pane window, for example, is slow going and exacting work. If you're with the majority, you can avoid scratching the paint by wrapping a rag (we use an old glove) around the tips of the ladder placed against the siding, while you do the top half of the window. If you scratch the sill, you can easily retouch by opening the window from inside the house. Obviously, there's no problem if the painter is using a scaffold or when you're on the ground level, even if you have to use a stepladder to reach the top part of the windows.

Never close windows tightly after painting them; leave the upper and lower sashes slightly ajar. After the paint has dried, work them up and down a few times. Do this for the next three days to prevent sticking. To help make the windows slide easily, apply a small amount of silicone spray to the sides.

Another point to keep in mind when caulking combination windows: don't caulk over the "weep holes" at the bottom of the storm window. These are ventilation holes that also allow water to escape. In fact, it's a good idea to use an awl or nail to make sure these weep holes are open on each window.

Gutters and Downspouts

It is generally better to paint gutters and downspouts the same color as the siding to blend in with the rest of the house, rather than allow them to stand out in contrast and appear to cut the house in pieces. It's also much easier than trying to paint behind them without smearing the enameled surface of the downspout, and easier than removing the fixtures completely and trying to get a snug fit when you replace them.

Porches and Steps

Your porch should be tied into the house color scheme; either the same or a contrasting color. (Make sure that you include this area when you figure the total square footage for your paint pur-

chase.) If it's the same color, you can use the same primer and finish paint on the rails and siding. If it's a contrasting color, it will probably be the same color as the trim, and here also, you can use the same paint. The porch floor and steps, however, are somewhat different. The primer can be the same as your house or trim primer, but your finish coat should be a special Deck Paint. This is usually available in a dozen or so basic colors and is specially formulated to stand up under weather abuse and foot traffic.

When first applied, deck paint is very slippery because of the high gloss and consequently dangerous when wet. Morning and evening dew can be especially treacherous, because you can't see the film of water on the surface. To overcome this you can add an anti-slip compound to the paint. This additive is a very fine, sand-like powder and can be stirred right into the paint. (It's often used on small and pleasure craft boat decks.) Ask your dealer about it.

Foundations

We call the foundation "blockwork" and consider it to be almost as important as the siding. If you skip it (or even the cellar windows), the rest of the house could look shabby despite your good work on the siding.

In older homes, the foundations are often made of stone. If it has never been painted and it's properly tuckpointed, leave it as is. But if the material is cement block, poured concrete, or block covered with stucco, it will probably look better if it's painted, especially if much of the foundation shows. Whatever the material, it is usually much rougher than the siding, so it's best to use a flat paint. We usually use an exterior flat latex and tint the shade needed to blend into the body of the house or to contrast with it. If two coats are needed, use the same paint. If your foundation looks good with one coat, move on to the cellar windows.

Shutters

Remove them before you start to paint your siding primer coat and store them on the porch or some closed off area; save them for a rainy day when you can't work on the siding. When you remove them, make sure that you label each one individually. Shutters are hand-fitted, and often not every one will fit each window.

We usually mark each shutter to match the window. We hammer our screwdriver blade on the top edge of the shutter to make a Roman numeral: I, II, III, etc. We put that same numeral on the face of the casing underneath the shutter hook. We can then look up from the ground to see the numeral and pick out the shutter that matches it.

It is important that the shutter paint be non-chalking, particularly if you're using a contrasting trim or if your siding is natural brick or stone. Chalking paint could be unsightly. The same rules apply to wooden shutters as to the rest of the trim: two coats of paint — one primer and one finish.

Doors

Your front entrance, especially the front door, will probably receive a closer inspection than any other part of the house. We generally paint all of the doors at one time, making sure that there are no lumps of dirt in the paint by screening it, if necessary, through an old wire screen. Screening the paint is usually unnecessary when painting toward the top of the house, but we do make certain that everything at ground level looks clean.

Most front doors are painted the same color as the rest of the trim but some, depending on the type of door, will need a stain or natural wood covering. If your door falls into this last category, see Chapter 9: Staining.

EXTERIOR SURFACES
Aluminum Siding

In recent years, improvements have been made in the life of the paint covering of steel and aluminum siding. Some companies even offer twenty year or even lifetime limited warranties. Even so, and this is especially true of the older aluminum siding now in place, many may need to be repainted after about twelve years. (The manufacturer's warranty can tell you more about specifics, but even a casual inspection should tell you if it needs painting.)

Aluminum siding can be painted exactly as wood siding. No special paint is needed. Wash down the chalk, scrape the chipped part, and apply a primer coat, followed by a finish coat of paint. The finish coat can be either latex or oil, but the prime coat should be an oil base paint.

Brick

If your brick house (or side) has already been painted, there's no decision; eventually it must be repainted. If it is still natural brick, think carefully before painting because it is next to impossible to remove the paint once it's on the siding. New brick carries paint better than used brick because there are fewer bleeding salts and acids to affect the paint. However, brick can be painted successfully and we do it often. Flat latex is better than a glossy oil finish. We've found that oil finish tends to highlight the imperfections, whereas flat latex has a tendency to hide them. Use two coats of flat latex. The easiest way to paint brick is with a long nap roller or by spraying.

Wood Shingles

You face a similar situation if you have shingle siding. Once painted, there's no returning to natural shingle. If you decide to paint or if it needs repainting, the same rule applies here as to wood siding, regarding oil vs. latex paint. If your shingles will be white, use an oil base primer and finish. If a color, use an oil base primer and a latex finish.

Natural (unpainted) shingles should be treated with a wood preservative. A note of caution here — not about using the wood preservative, but the penalties of not using it. Some homeowners want a "weathered" look exterior and avoid using any coating at all on their shingle siding. As a result, particularly on the south side but essentially any exposed side, the sun will turn the shingles black in spots. It looks ugly because it's an uneven, mottled effect and once it's there, only two coats of paint will completely cover it.

Wood shingles need protection against the elements. You can purchase "natural" stain and still protect the shingles or the wood siding. This "sunburned" effect will also occur if you wait too long before reapplying stain. So keep a weather eye out, or more appropriately, an eye on the weathered-out side of your siding. And since staining is usually easier than painting, do it sooner than later.

Asbestos Shingles

Many houses in the East, especially those built during the Depression years, have asbestos shingles. They're a problem to paint because they have a tendency to deteriorate on the sunny sides of the house. They puff up to expose the fiber, a condition we call "punky."

We examine each side of the house and scrape a fingernail along a leading edge. If we can scrape off any of the asbestos fibers, we apply a special surface conditioner before painting. This is a mixture of oils and driers that dry and harden, effectively turning the soft and "punky" surface to a hard surface that will accept paint. We lightly sand the raised surface and rough spots, then apply two coats of flat latex finish, or a latex primer and a flat latex finish.

Stucco

Stucco is a mixture of cement, sand, and lime that usually has a rough, pebble-like texture which can be painted or left in a natural condition. If the surface has deteriorated or is soft and crumbly to your fingernails, you should use a masonry conditioner, then apply a flat latex paint of whatever color you choose. Since it's a flat paint, you can use a second coat if you feel it's needed. Stucco is best painted with a long nap roller or sprayer.

NOTE: Often stucco just needs to be washed rather than painted. The best way to do this is with a power washer.

Asphalt Shingles

It's possible to paint asphalt shingles, but you should use a latex paint because the asphalt tar tends to bleed and latex will retard this condition better than oil paint.

ONE COAT VS. TWO COATS

A while ago, a man came into our paint store and said, "I want you guys to come out to look at my house. Then I want you to go to court with me and testify that I did a good paint job on the house."

I don't know whether it was me or one of my sons who said, "Huh?" So he went on to explain that it was a long story but . . . "My wife and I just got a divorce. Part of the settlement was to have the house painted. So I painted the house myself. My ex says that I did a lousy job and that she's going to sue me if I don't have the house painted right. That's why I want you guys, who are experts, to go to court and tell the judge it's a good job."

We didn't go, in fact, we hadn't even sold him the paint so I can't be sure just what paint he did use, but I'd be willing to bet that I know what happened. And this leads into another incident.

Recently a man called our paint store and wanted to know the cost of paint and how to go about using it. He said that he had never done any painting in his life but that he was planning on painting his house. Rather than try to explain on the phone, I drove over to his house.

I went over the whole story with him and explained what paint he should use and why he needed two coats. I also explained that I didn't make a practice of house calls for people who buy paint, but that I didn't want him to get into trouble since he knew very little about painting. I also said that I did expect him to stop by the store and buy our paint when he decided to start, and that we'd help him as his job progressed. Next day, he stopped in the store. I was out, but my son Jimmy explained the entire story to him again. The following day he stopped by again, and this time we were both in. He kept talking about one coat and still didn't buy any paint. After he left and we talked it over, I knew that he wouldn't return because he wanted us to tell him that he really only needed one coat. And I knew that he'd buy latex paint because we had told him that it's easier to clean up. Fortunately, he couldn't get into any trouble because his existing paint was latex. So all that could happen was that his work wouldn't look great (even if he used the same color) and that he'd have to repaint in a year or so because his house was long overdue for a paint job.

My point is this: There are people who simply hate to paint and won't pay to have it done. So when the house desperately needs painting (often the bank insists that it be painted to protect their mortgage investment, or the man's wife threatens to leave unless the house is cleaned up), the poor guy finds himself backed into a corner with nothing to do but paint. He isn't looking for a feeling of accomplishment or aesthetics, he just wants it over with. And he couldn't care less about long-lasting protection. What he wants is a shortcut. Which translates into one coat of paint, usually latex because it's easier. And that's where he could get himself into trouble.

Please understand that we are not opposed to one coat painting jobs. We often paint a house where a single coat on the body of the house is sufficient. Usually, on this same house, we will need two coats on the trim which somehow seems to take more of a beating than the siding. However, most often it is advisable to use two coats of paint on a house exterior: a primer and a finish coat. The use of a primer means better adhesion for the finish coat, a more uniform finish coat, and better, longer lasting protection.

In this chapter I've tried to explain how to do it right, so this is a short course on how to keep out of trouble if you do take the shortcut.

First, you can't put just any new paint over any old existing paint. You can apply new latex over old (or existing) latex because latex chalks very little if it has a flat finish. So you can buy another can of flat latex finish and put it on top of the existing latex finish. To get away with one coat, your new paint should be pretty much the same color as the existing paint.

You can also put an oil base paint over existing latex. You can put a new oil paint over existing oil paint, but you'll probably need a primer coat. And you'll almost certainly need a primer if you put latex on existing oil paint.

Oil base paints chalk, and oil base paints usually have a glossy or shiny finish. And you can't put a finish coat over these conditions without first putting on a primer coat. To make a finish coat stick on a shiny surface, you must sand it first and that, believe me, ain't no fun. (Imagine trying to sand the shine off a porch ceiling.)

That's why we automatically prime the shiny spots, even if we're doing a one coat job on the rest of the siding.

I have used the phrase "getting into trouble" to

describe what happens if you don't follow the basic rules. What will happen is nothing like causing your roof to leak or your windows to fall out. What will happen is that your paint will start to peel and you'll soon have to do the job over. Which means that you'll have to repeat the performance that you hated to do in the first place. But if you do it right, you can forget about it for another half dozen years. Maybe by that time your kids will help.

Let's go back to trim — and the reason for two coats. The areas around the windows may be banged up if you have removable screens and storm windows, especially if they have to be pried off. Other parts will be shiny. Both conditions need a coat of primer before you apply the finish coat.

SUMMARY

After prime coat has been applied:

- Box finish paint (if using a color); paint from work bucket.

- Fill cracks or holes with putty or caulking as you come to them.

- Best procedure is to paint windows after siding is painted and dry.

- Paint gutters and downspouts the same color as the siding.

- Tie porch into house color scheme, but paint floor and steps with deck paint for longer wear.

- Identify shutters before removing.

- Treat aluminum siding as wood if it needs painting.

- Don't neglect wood shingles to achieve "natural" look. Use wood preservative or appropriate stain.

- If brick house has not been painted, consider carefully before applying paint. There's no turning back after painting.

- Don't shortcut preparation or prime coat.

5
Interior Painting

EQUIPMENT NEEDED

- ☐ Dropcloth (cloth or plastic sheeting)
- ☐ Paintbrush kit
- ☐ Roller
- ☐ Roller tray
- ☐ Paint
- ☐ Bucket, detergent, sponge
- ☐ Newspaper
- ☐ Clean cloths (for wiping hands, cleaning spills)
- ☐ Spackle or plaster and spackle knife (if patching needed)
- ☐ Stain (if staining trim)
- ☐ Sandpaper & steel wool
- ☐ Stepladder
- ☐ Putty (if needed)
- ☐ Masking tape (preferably painter's tape)

Just about every adult and probably most teenagers have painted or assisted in painting a room. So you already know it's not all that difficult, but it is time consuming, especially if you do it right. However, if you follow professional procedure, the finished job is rewarding, attractive, and long lasting.

Many of the mass merchandising stores carry several lines of paint and each line offers a variety of choices, both interior and exterior. Consequently, the display is apt to be a bit awesome unless you have a pretty good idea of what you want. So please, at this point review Chapter 1: About Paint. Knowing what to look for will save you time and probably save you money.

Before you purchase your paint, you should know how much you'll need. The rule of thumb we use at the paint store when a customer asks, "How much will I need?" is:

- Four walls of an average room (12′ × 15′ × 8½′ high) equals one gallon of paint. If your room is bigger than average, buy a gallon plus an additional quart. If you have paint left over, keep it for touch up.

- Two ceilings equal one gallon (one coat). If you're painting the ceiling the same color as the walls, use the same paint. (But buy at least a gallon and a half.) NOTE: Two quarts will probably cost almost as much as a gallon.

■ One quart of paint will usually do the trim (woodwork). That is one quart of enamel undercoater, based on a typical room with two doors, two windows, and baseboards. You also need a quart of enamel finish paint. (Trim generally requires two coats.)

Unlike exterior painting, which usually calls for primer and finish coats, one interior coat might be sufficient for your walls when redecorating unless you are changing the color. If so, you're probably not going to get away with just one coat. Also, in many instances, your first coat would use the same paint as your second coat. You might not know for sure if you will need a second coat, so buy only enough paint for the first coat. Make sure you keep the formula so that you can duplicate the shade if you do need two coats. If you do, order it when you run out of the first batch. However, if it looks like you will run out of paint, finish to the corner and then stop. Don't switch paints in the middle of a wall. If you stop in the corner and start off the next corner with another can of matching paint, you'll never know the difference, even if the match is off a bit. If your paint is custom mixed, it might not match exactly. Even factory-mixed paints can vary slightly from batch to batch.

The warning is worth repeating: Never stop in the middle of a wall or a ceiling and go out to get more paint. You will see the overlap if you do.

Make sure the paint is well stirred before using. Even if you just had it shaken at the paint shop yesterday, it still settles out. But before you start to paint, you should wash the walls. And before you wash the walls, move the furniture into the middle of the room, and remove the objects from the walls. Don't take off the switch plates until you finish washing.

REPAINTING A ROOM

Let's say an average living room is about 12′ × 15′ × 8½′ high. A handy homeowner or apartment dweller husband and wife team should be able to paint it one coat during a weekend — four workdays. That includes washing the ceiling, walls, and trim; patching them if needed; painting the ceiling, walls, and woodwork. I say team because two people can usually do more than twice as much work as one person, and some of the work, such as moving furniture, usually requires two people.

Incidentally, all of the above is predicated on the premise that everything is ready to go. If you have to spend most of Saturday morning buying paint and looking for brushes, ladders, and dropcloths all bets are off.

Preparation

You must move the furniture so that you can walk around to get at the walls and the ceiling. It's best if you can move the furniture out of the room, but if there's a heavy couch or large table, move it to the center of the room and cover it well. We use canvas dropcloths, which are best, but you can also use plastic sheets.

CAUTION: Plastic sheets are dangerous to use on the floor, especially the flimsy kind. They have a tendency to slide out from under you which could easily cause a fall.

Before you lay down your dropcloths, cover whatever furniture you leave in the room with newspapers, several pages thick, especially on the flat surfaces. We've learned from long experience that it's easier to put down a paint bucket or a hammer on top of something than it is to put it on the floor. (You shouldn't, but then you don't have to bend down so far if you do.) However, this could cause a scratch or dent on your furniture and the newspaper cushion will give you added protection. Finally, lay down layers of newspaper wherever there's a bare spot on the floor that a dropcloth doesn't cover.

Walls and Ceiling

When the furniture has been removed or well covered, wash the walls and ceilings with a solution of Spic 'N Span, Soilex, or other detergent and water. This is not to imply that your home has dirty walls; what we're mostly concerned about is grease from the kitchen and smoke stain from cigarettes and/or a fireplace. Over a period of years smoke accumulates on the ceiling primarily, but also on parts of the walls. If there is an obvious smoke-stained area and you attempt to paint over it, the stain will continue to discolor through the new paint, regardless of the number of coats of latex paint you apply. The solution is to use a "stain kill" on the spot or area. Failing that, you can use an oil base undercoater or flat oil paint. When it's dry you can paint over it with your latex paint. If the stain is extensive, cover the entire ceiling with a flat oil base paint.

You should always wash the woodwork. You can use the same cleaning solution. (For woodwork, we use a liquid cleaner called Will Bond made by the Imperial Company. It's also called a "liquid sandpaper.") Your main purpose in cleaning woodwork is to remove the wax, but it's also to dull the surface to allow a better bond for the paint.

After washing, we remove the hardware in the room: the plates from around the doorknobs, switch plates, and window locks. If there are brass outlet plates, they can be polished up like new by boiling them in a solution of vinegar and water for three to five minutes. Then go over them lightly with a fine grade of steel wool. Plastic outlet plates can be cleaned with soap and water or painted.

NOTE: Do not remove the electrical outlet plates before you wash the walls.

Next we prepare the walls and ceilings by filling the cracks, sanding, and taking care of any openings between the door casings or baseboard and the wall. A fine crack — up to 1/8″ wide — can be filled with mixed spackle right from the can. First, run the sandpaper down the crack, then dust out the residue with a dust brush, or you can use an old flexible paint brush as a duster. Apply the spackle with your knife to fill the crack. When the spackle is dry, sand it smooth flush with the wall, repeat if necessary, then dust. Don't bother to spackle hairline cracks. Just sand lightly and the dust residue will fill in the crack. After sanding, dust the area around the crack clean.

Cracks that are larger than 1/8″ should be cut out (a "church key" can opener works fine) and filled in with patching plaster. It's better not to use plaster of paris because that dries too rapidly. After you have cleaned it out, run your sandpaper down the sides of the crack to allow a nice, smooth track for your patching plaster. Then wet it well. When you have pressed your plaster into the open crack, take off the excess by running your spackle knife down the length of the crack. If you haven't sanded it first, the loose, dried paint and dirt in the crack will prevent you from filling the crack smoothly and will leave an uneven residue instead of a smooth patch. After applying your plaster, sand it smooth and dust it clean. An important note about plaster: Before you apply patching plaster, wet the surface you're working on with plain water. You can use a sponge or an old paintbrush. Fresh plaster applied to a dry surface won't stick well or last long. If you use spackle, do not wet the surface.

It's always better to build up slowly when filling a crack than to fill up the crack with too much plaster and have to sand it down. The professionals put on two or three fillings and build up gradually to avoid having to sand off a ridge to make it level with the rest of the wall.

You can use paste spackle on woodwork. Just apply the spackle on small cracks and use a damp cloth to wipe the area. This will force the spackle into the crack. You won't even have to wait for the spackle to dry because it's now formulated so that you can paint right over it. It's best to use wood

Scrape a crack smooth before filling it with spackle. This can be done with sandpaper or a knife or both.

Larger cracks should be opened with a stiff knife or a church key can opener. Brush the crack clean before filling with spackle.

This is the result of a bad leak in the ceiling. The plaster is cracked, the paper has peeled, and a chunk of plaster has fallen out of the ceiling. The first thing to do, of course, is to stop the leak, then repair the damage. The hole will take at least two fillings.

When you patch a large hole in the wall or ceiling, keep your first filling of plaster shallow, then make your second filling flush with the wall.

You can use a hook scraper; or a stiff putty knife, shown here, to scrape off loose paint, but don't gouge the wood.

This is the proper way to hold a flexible spackle knife. These are small but deep holes in a plaster wall.

This is a good — or bad — example of chipping paint. This paint was applied over a coat of hard, glossy varnish which should have been removed first.

filler or caulking compound for a larger crack in woodwork. Remember to sand and dust before painting.

This is personal, but I think that most professional painters feel the same. To me, nothing looks worse than a freshly painted room with gaps between the wall and door casings or top of the baseboard. I like everything tightened up. These gaps can easily be filled in with paste spackle, patching plaster, or caulk. As long as you're doing it, do it right.

You'll find it's more convenient to do the woodwork patching at the same time that you do the walls and ceiling. (You'll remember, on the exterior I advised you to do patching after the primer.)

Ready to Paint

You'll need both a roller (with an extension pole) and tray for paint, a brush with a separate paint bucket, and a stepladder or step stool.

Do the ceiling first. Start at the narrow end of the room and work across the back, then down the length of the room. Here is where your teamwork pays off. One person cuts in with a brush and the other rolls the paint on the ceiling. Virtually all non-professionals handle this procedure wrong. The following is the right way.

Cut in the ceiling only (not ceiling and wall) by painting with your brush a 2″ or 3″ wide band along the place where the ceiling meets the wall. (The roller won't reach here.) Paint a strip about two feet long. Then roll the ceiling paint along this strip. Now brush on another two foot strip and roll on the ceiling paint. You keep the edges wet by painting in small portions. If you're working with a partner, one cuts in, the other rolls on. Otherwise you're putting down the brush and picking up the roller again and again and again.

Most people cut in the entire ceiling before rolling, and often cut in the wall at the same time. However, if you do that your paint will dry and you'll

have a lap, or two coats of paint, all around the edges. Since the paint is twice as heavy here, it very often shows through. With a little practice, the person cutting in can stay just ahead of the person rolling the ceiling.

Here's another "don't" — and it's probably the non-professional painter's biggest sin. Don't roll out the paint too much. You won't notice until the paint has dried and then you'll see that the paint hasn't really covered in certain spots, which means that you'll have to apply another coat.

When we sell wall and ceiling paint at our shop, we often tell our customers, "Don't paint more than two or three feet with a roller full of paint." Then, after they respond with, "Huh?", we explain why. The words "apply liberally" appear on the labels of most latex paints. The advice is not given in order to sell more paint. It's to make sure you cover properly.

After doing the ceiling, repeat the procedure on the walls, completing one at a time. One coat could be all that's necessary if you have a fairly close match with the existing color and if there is little or no patching involved. You cannot paint white over a dark color (or the reverse) with a single coat. Your first few strokes on the wall should indicate whether or not you need a second coat. If the previous color does show through and you do need a second coat, it's not a big problem because you can use the same paint, provided it is a flat latex paint. Most wall and ceiling paint is flat latex and a self-primer, because most people don't want high gloss walls. You can even hold to your weekend schedule because most latex paints are recoatable in two hours.

An Additional Note About Ceilings

Older homes usually have plaster ceilings; new houses are probably drywall, although some have textured spray foam or suspended ceiling tile. Actually, all kinds of building materials are used for

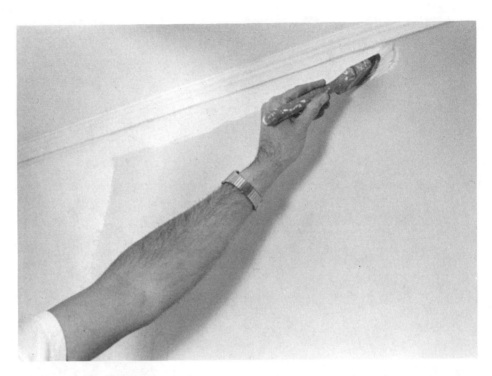

This is the proper way to cut in. Paint two or three feet with a brush along the ceiling, then roll the wall.

After the wall along the ceiling is cut in, roll the wall. It's best to work a small area at a time and roll it back and forth into the finished area.

Use a full roll of paint to work back into the finished area to make sure that there will not be an overlap or skipped space.

Cutting in along the door casing. Only a small part of the door casing and ceiling is cut in before rolling. This is so the cut-in portion won't dry and cause an overlap.

ceilings. Even so, apart from cracks, which should be repaired with spackle or patching plaster before painting, there are usually two potential trouble spots. Both of them are stains: smoke and water.

If there's a water stain, you know it's there because it has probably turned black or yellow at the edges. You might not be so aware of smoke stains unless you've had a fire. But if your room has a fireplace, or has had at least one smoker in the family for a number of years, the ceiling has probably picked up a yellowish tinge.

Both smoke and water stains must be treated before painting or the stains will come through the next coat of latex paint. Step one is to wash the ceiling. You use the same detergent solution that you used to wash the walls. However, washing alone won't always remove the stains. Step two is a coat of flat, oil base paint. Not latex, oil base, which offers much better protection against the stains coming through. If you only have a small stain, or you don't want to wait until the next day when the oil paint dries, you can use a "stain killer." We sell two brands; one called Enamelac, a pigmented white shellac, and the other called Wipeout (Oxline Paint Co.), a naphtha base product. (They have a strong odor but they work.) These dry fast — a half hour at most — and can be painted over with your latex paint, effectively covering the stain. (Stain killers are popular with professional painters because they do dry so fast, whereas oil paint covering a stain takes overnight to dry.)

PAINTING TRIM

This includes windows, doors, baseboards, and kitchen cabinets — all the woodwork. It's safer to use two coats of paint on the trim. Sorry about that. Worse, walls and ceiling go quickly, trim doesn't. Especially windows.

Don't use your wall and ceiling paint on the woodwork because you need an enamel undercoater.

This is a flat paint, either oil or latex, that has been formulated to stick on the existing paint and to provide a bond for your finish coat, which should be a semi-gloss (or satin) finish enamel. And, of course, both paints should be tinted to the color you've selected.

NOTE: If you prefer, instead of a latex enamel finish paint, you can just as well use an oil base enamel finish over the latex undercoater on the woodwork. However, as mentioned earlier, the oil base paint does have a slight odor that could last for several days, and it's more difficult to clean up.

Windows

You paint windows, like everything else, from the top down. But when you are painting a double hung window (this is the standard two-part window that slides up and down) you must move the bottom up and the top down to paint the overlap. We usually paint the overlap first (we call it the "parting strip") thus handling the windows while they're dry, and then the upper sash, followed by the lower sash, before painting the casing. (The sash is the frame that holds the glass; the casing is the side and front pieces that separate the window from the wall. The sill is the horizontal piece at the bottom of the frame.)

The window sill is painted last. It's a good idea to wipe off the sill with a rag followed by a couples of swipes with a piece of sandpaper just before painting to make sure that you're not covering over any lumps or droplets of paint from the upper portions of the window.

When finished, leave the windows slightly open from the top and bottom to prevent sticking. When our painters come back the next day, before we close the windows we work them up and down a few times. Do this for three days after you've applied the finish coat and they'll never stick. A few drops of silicone sprayed along the sash run will also help them to slide smoothly. If they're

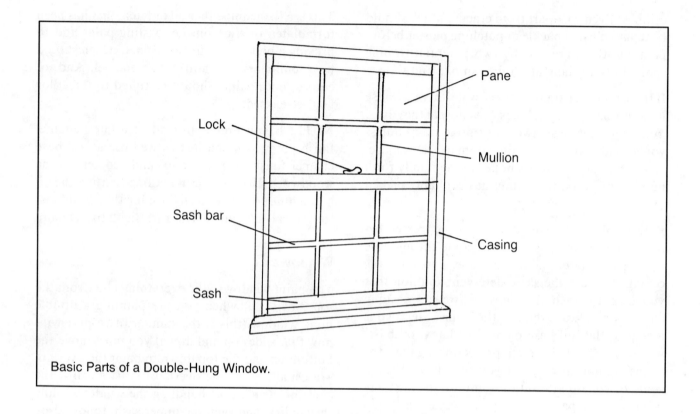

Basic Parts of a Double-Hung Window.

Double-Hung Windows

Vinyl replacement window units often supply plastic grids to convert a standard two-pane window into the colonial, twelve-light style shown here. These don't need painting. However, unless your home has been built (or remodeled) in the last few years, you'll have to paint or stain your windows.

Sill — Bottom part of the window. The interior sill is flat; the outside sill is slanted to allow precipitation to run off.

Casing — Generally the window frame, or that part in which the window is hung.

Sash — The frame that holds the glass.

Pane — The window glass. Also called Light.

Mullion — Vertical bars that hold the glass in place. Not in standard style windows.

Sash Bar — The horizontal crosspiece.

Lock — The two-part metal unit that secures the bottom sash to the top.

The painter is using a dark grey paint over an existing light color; note that the metal fixtures have been removed. Paint the lower half of the upper sash, as indicated. Then push it up to its original position and paint the top half. Next do the lower sash.

The 2½" angled brush is best, but you can also use a 2" brush, either angled or straight. Holding the brush as indicated gives you good control with trim.

stuck shut before you start, you can cut them loose top and bottom with a putty knife. If they still won't break free, you might have to use your putty knife on the outside, cutting the paint along the sides and bottom of the sash. Then, with someone pushing up from the outside and someone else from the inside, it has to open. Unless it's nailed shut.

A handy device to help you paint the frames without smearing the glass is called a "straight edge": essentially a rigid strip of plastic about 8″ long. (You can get one at any paint or hardware store.) Lay this on the glass and press against the frame as you stroke your brush and you'll keep the line neat and the glass clean. Clean off the plastic guide to prevent a buildup of paint. If you do get paint on the glass, wipe it up before it hardens. If it does harden, you can easily scrape it off with a scraper blade or a single edge razor blade.

There is also a product called Liquid Masking Tape which is painted on the glass before you paint the window. Then, when it dries, you can paint the window without fear of slopping paint on the glass because the liquid mask just pulls off. However, you must apply it carefully because if you get any on the window frame, the paint won't stick.

Thus far, we have been talking about painting the windows with a bristle brush. Some people prefer a "poly brush" applicator, which is really a small piece of polyester foam, usually cut to a chisel edge, affixed to a handle or piece of doweling. They come in 1″, 2″, 3″, and 4″ sizes and if these give you better control, by all means use them. Another good feature is that they're inexpensive and can be disposable.

A number of our customers say they prefer poly brushes for varnish work because their brushes leave bristles on the surface. We seldom make a point of explaining that the reason the brush leaves bristles is that it's worn out or old and shedding.

Doors

Before painting, make sure that you have newspapers under the door to catch any drip or spray. We paint the door first on both sides, then the casing. Use a brush for the doors, not the roller, and paint with the grain of the wood. People seem to notice doors more than any other part of the house, so try to do an especially good job here. After you apply the primer coat, make sure the paint is dry before putting on the finish coat. A latex primer coat should dry in about two hours but use the fingernail test to make sure; run your fingernail along the newly painted surface. If you pick up paint, it's still wet. (You'll also have to clean your fingernails.)

The standard procedure for painting a door is:

■ paint the edge first, wiping off the other side of the door when finished;

■ starting at the top, paint each of the panels;

■ then the cross pieces;

■ and finally the stiles — the vertical sides that hold the panels.

If it's a solid door, start at the top and work down, laying off with the grain of the wood.

Watch out for "runs" when you're painting a door. When most people finish painting the door they walk away from it thinking, "Okay, that's done." Not so, and don't do it. Check back in two or three minutes to pick up the possible streamers of paint. Many, if not most, doors have molding, especially paneled doors. The grooves in the molding capture an excess of paint which begins to run in a few minutes. Runs make your beautiful paint job look non-professional.

There is a standard procedure to cover a situation where the door is painted one color on one side and another color on the other. If there is disagreement at your home as to which color goes with which room, and to avoid a letter to Miss Manners, the

When painting a door hold the brush comfortably, as indicated, and do the panel first, laying off with the grain of wood.

After the panel (or panels) has been painted, do the edges of the door, then start at the top and do the stiles. Lay off with the grain of wood, horizontally with the top piece and vertically at the sides. Paint one unit at a time. The painter shown here is using a 3" brush but a 2½" brush would work just as well.

rule is this: when the door is closed, it should be the same color as the rest of the trim in that room. For example, let's say the bedroom is green and the adjacent hall is white. When closed, the bedroom side of the door would be green and the hall side would be white. You should do this even though these colors would be reversed when the door was open and it probably would be open most of the time. If all of this seems to make life too difficult, it is perfectly acceptable to paint both sides the same color, usually going with the bedroom color, as in our example above.

One final note on doors. Sometimes doors are painted on one side and stained on the other. If you are faced with this situation, remember to do the staining first and the painting second. After staining, apply at least one coat of varnish, then do the painted side. This is so you'll be able to remove any paint spots from the stained area.

Kitchen Cabinets

As we have mentioned, it's important to wash the woodwork before painting any trim. It's absolutely essential with woodwork in the kitchen. This is because you must clean wax from wood; paint won't adhere to wax. Even if you don't intentionally use wax, many cleaners have wax as one of the ingredients. In addition, woodwork in the kitchen collects cooking grease.

Kitchen cabinets with a varnished finish are especially tricky to paint over because paint doesn't bond well on a varnished surface. Time was when you had to remove the varnish first before you could paint. Now it's a lot easier because several products on the market nicely solve this problem. We use one called Between Coat made by McCloskey or LSP — Liquid Surface Preparation. This is applied after the varnished surface has been thoroughly washed and sanded. After dusting, we put on the clear liquid, let dry for about thirty minutes, and then apply the undercoat while the surface is still tacky. The two coats will dry together and provide a good bond for your finish coat.

Baseboards

After everything else in the room is covered with an undercoat, we paint the baseboards. We also apply the finish coat on the baseboards last. That's because there's more dirt in this area than any other, probably because it's next to the floor where dirt collects. Make it a point to do the rest of the woodwork before starting on the baseboards. Unless you do, you'll be transferring the dirt up to the window or the door.

After you finish the baseboards, if you plan to use the same paint in another room, strain the paint before you start on the new work. We use pantyhose for this. Stretch the pantyhose above a fresh, clean bucket and pour the paint onto it. It should be tied off so that the sag doesn't drag into the paint. Don't stir or force the draining. When finished, wrap a newspaper around the pantyhose and dispose of it. If you are without access to pantyhose, you can buy paint strainers that fit over the top of the paint can.

If your room has wall-to-wall carpet, you might have some difficulty in getting down below the carpet level. This is where you use your straight edge. Press the edge on top of the carpet and run your brush along the plastic strip. Wipe off the straight edge after each move. Do that all the way around the room and you'll never have a drop of paint on the carpet.

We should touch on a special condition frequently found in older houses, namely lumps and sags in the woodwork caused during a previous painting. Painting over them only perpetuates the condition. The solution is to use a dull chisel and dig the lump out. It is infinitely easier than trying to sand it down, even with a belt sander. (Don't use a circular sander on woodwork because it will leave swirls in the wood.) When you dig out the lump, fill it in with spackle, sand smooth, and paint over for a nice smooth surface.

If there's a large opening, a gouge, or even a piece of wood missing, we use a water putty that comes as a dry powder in a can. When mixed with water it can be molded over the damaged part of the woodwork. It quickly dries very hard and should be sanded and dusted before painting.

There is also a special condition found in older homes, especially on doors and baseboards. This is a chipping or cracking condition that occurred several (or many) paintings ago and was painted over. In addition to looking unsightly, the chipping will continue every time you hit the area, with the vacuum cleaner at the baseboard, for example. New paint will not hold old paint in place. The remedy is to chip the paint down to a solid base with a dull putty knife, or better still, use paint and varnish remover and remove the old paint.

Finally, after the paint has dried, you can take your hardware, polish the brass with fine steel wool, and replace. So now your room is finished. (After you put the furniture back.) And just in time for dinner.

COMMON QUESTIONS ABOUT INTERIOR PAINTING

Q. *What is the best paint to use in a bathroom or kitchen?*

A. Either alkyd or latex enamel because the smooth finish is easy to clean and resists moisture and grease.

Q. *Can I use latex wall paint on woodwork?*

A. Yes, but if the woodwork is subject to heavy wear, an enamel is preferable.

Q. *Can I get the same color in wall paint and enamel for trim and woodwork?*

A. Yes, but the gloss finish of enamel will cause it to look slightly different than the flat finish of the wall paint.

Q. *What's the best way to select a color of interior paint?*

A. Take the color samples home and view them in both natural light and the existing room light.

Q. *How can I paint a room to look larger or smaller?*

A. Light colors will make a room appear larger. Dark colors will make a room look smaller.

Q. *If I buy more of a color later, will it match?*

A. Always buy enough paint before you begin. However, if you think you're going to run out, always stop painting in a corner. If you stop in the middle of a wall, the difference will be obvious.

Q. *What's the difference between ceiling and wall paint?*

A. Ceiling paint minimizes surface defects and reflects light. It is not designed for heavy washing.

Q. *What is the best time of year to paint a room?*

A. Anytime is okay, but good air circulation in the room (i.e., open windows) speeds up the drying time and minimizes odor.

PAINTING A PANELED ROOM

Many years ago it was fashionable to panel a room to add a distinctive touch of class to the interior. However, through the years, in many homes the paneling has become darker and darker, until now the room is sometimes just plain gloomy. If you have such a room, you don't have to tear out the paneling and replace it because it's quite simple to paint over it with a lighter color. It's amazing how quickly this can change the character of the room and restore the original touch of class.

The procedure is much the same as any other re-painting except that you'll need three coats of paint: enamel undercoater and enamel finish, either latex or oil base. First, clean the surface to get rid of dirt and especially wax. You can use a warm water and detergent solution. Or you can use (and we recommend) a commercial cleaner such as Will Bond. This dries very rapidly and can be painted over almost immediately.

When the surface is dry, apply your undercoat. After that dries, apply the second coat of under-coat. Then your enamel finish coat. Just make sure that the paint is dry between coats. Remember that paint dries more slowly near the windows, so use the fingernail test.

Whenever we do one of these interiors, the owners invariably say, "This looks great! I wonder why we didn't do it years ago."

PAINTING A NEW ROOM

This is the procedure that we use and recommend that you follow to paint a new room after the carpenters have finished. The drywall surfaces have been taped and everything is ready for painting. (The procedure is the same if your walls and ceiling are plaster.)

First, you should clean the room thoroughly with a vacuum cleaner; everything, including the window sills and even the walls if they appear to be dusty. There is no need to cover the floor because you either have a rough floor (and you intend to lay wall-to-wall carpeting) or a hardwood floor that has yet to be sanded and finished. In either event, the floor is done after the painting.

Most times we will use three coats of paint on the walls and ceiling. You might possibly get away with two coats but plan on three. (More on this later.) You will certainly have to use three coats on the new woodwork.

I recommend you use a latex undercoater and a latex finish for the walls and ceiling. For the wood-work, either a latex or oil undercoater and an enamel, semi-gloss or satin finish; again, either latex or oil base.

To keep the procedure as simple as possible, the kinds of paint you will need are as follows:

For Walls and Ceiling

☐ Latex Interior Undercoat — For first two coats; tinted to same color as finish.

☐ Latex Wall and Ceiling Finish — For final coat; tinted to exact color you choose.

For Woodwork

☐ Latex or Oil Enamel Undercoater — For first two coats; tinted.

☐ Semi-Gloss Enamel Finish — For final coat; tinted to exact color you choose; either latex or oil base.

When all of your equipment is in place, start with your undercoater on the ceiling and apply with a roller. However, follow the same procedure (see REPAINTING A ROOM on page 38) of cutting in along the ceiling with a brush, one small section at a time. Here again, a two person team works best; one cutting, the other rolling.

Expect to have your first coat look awful. The paint will cover some areas of the bare drywall and sink into others, but don't worry, the next coat will smooth things out. However, this condition is the reason that you'll probably have to use three coats.

After you finish the ceiling, continue with the walls. First, cut in along the top of the walls, then roll on a small section at a time. Keep the edges wet as you did with the ceiling.

It might seem easier to do the walls and ceiling first — all three coats — before you tackle the woodwork, but you should do the woodwork along with each coat of the walls and ceiling. That is, apply the first coat to the walls and ceiling, then the first coat on the woodwork; repeat the same procedure for the second coat and also the finish. Follow this routine even though you'll be using a different paint for the woodwork and probably a different color, which means that you'll have to clean your brush(es) each time you switch paints. The benefits are worth the inconvenience. You'll be far less likely to spill, slop, or spray your woodwork color on your nice, freshly finished walls with each application.

After everything has been painted with the first coat, you will notice that you have some tightening up to do. The white drywall may have looked nice and smooth before painting, but now you'll notice gouges and imperfections. Also cracks, nailholes, and spaces which should be spackled over are visible at this point. This is true of the woodwork as well as the walls.

As an experiment, run your hand over the nice, smooth, sanded but unpainted woodwork. Then do the same after your undercoat has dried. Now it feels almost as rough as sandpaper. That's because the paint has raised the fibers of the wood and they'll stay like that until you've sanded. There's no way you'll be able to run a dust cloth or mop along the baseboard until you do.

If the surface is curved or recessed, use steel wool; if flat, use a medium grade sandpaper. Incidentally, whichever you choose, wear a work glove to protect your hand. Steel wool especially has a way of twisting around and wearing down your fingernails to the quick. You can use the non-gloved hand to test the smoothness of your sanded steel wool work. You'll find it doesn't take much work to make it smooth.

After sanding the woodwork, fill the nailholes with putty. You can use any of the many brands of putty. Take a small amount from the can and roll it into a ball, then press the ball into the nailhole

and slide a flexible putty knife between your thumb and the ball of putty to cut it off flush at the hole's surface.

The next job is to clean out the room again with the vacuum cleaner and, if necessary, with a dust cloth on the walls. After cleaning, the progression is the same: paint the ceiling, walls, and then the woodwork, making sure that the baseboard is done last. Your first coat should dry in about two hours, but make sure that it really is dry before starting your primer coat. (Use the fingernail test to be sure.) However, one coat of paint on the ceiling, walls, and woodwork, plus sanding and tightening up, is a good day's work for a homeowner painter.

You'll notice that the second coat looks much better than the first. In fact, it might look so good that you'll wonder if you even need a third coat on the walls and ceiling. Before making that decision, look over the walls very carefully to make sure that there are not hollows or crevices to be filled. If there's any patching to be done, do it now because it's your last chance.

If at all possible, we recommend that you do apply the third coat because it will give you better and longer lasting protection, especially for washing the walls over the years you'll live with them.

Before starting your finish coat, run over the painted surface with your fingernail to see if any paint comes off. Check the windows especially to see if there is any soft paint. Cold or moist conditions around the windows could cause the paint in these areas to remain wet longer. When everything is dry, you'll have a solid bond with your finish coat.

The finish coat is handled by cutting in and rolling the ceiling, then the walls, exactly as you have applied the first two coats. When you are finished, you should sand the woodwork lightly before brushing on your finish coat, as you did before. Here again, paint the baseboard last.

After the paint is dry, put on the switch plates and window fixtures.

SUMMARY

To repaint a room:

■ Determine how much latex paint you will need. (See rule of thumb method on page 37.)

■ Wash ceiling and walls.

■ Fill cracks with spackle; sand and dust.

■ Paint ceiling first, then walls; cutting in along the ceiling a small strip at a time.

■ Paint two coats on trim: enamel undercoater and enamel finish.

To paint a new room:

■ Clean room and walls thoroughly.

■ Use three coats of latex paint on walls and ceiling; two undercoater, one finish.

■ Paint trim along with walls, three coats also; two enamel undercoater, one enamel finish.

6
Painting a Room with Wallpaper

EQUIPMENT NEEDED

- ☐ Lots of newspapers
- ☐ Scraper
- ☐ Garden sprayer (or bucket)
- ☐ Dropcloths
- ☐ Stepladder
- ☐ Paintbrush
- ☐ Roller
- ☐ Paint
- ☐ Spackle, plaster, or wall compound

The contemporary term for wallpaper is "wallcovering" because most of today's wallcoverings are made of vinyl rather than paper. However, in the trade the old-fashioned term is still used as the generic expression. I have used both words interchangeably and the salesperson will know what you're talking about if the term "wallpaper" is more comfortable for you.

IMPORTANT: Before doing anything, knock on the wall. If it sounds solid and makes a dull thud, it's plaster. And that's good. If it sounds hollow, it's drywall or wallboard. That might not be so good when it comes to removing wallcovering. Before attempting to remove wallcovering from drywall or wallboard, read the box below. Then, if you determine that conditions are favorable, proceed with the following instructions.

Proceed with caution before attempting to remove wallcovering if your walls are drywall or wallboard. If the wall has been properly prepared, the wallcovering should come off without damaging the wall. By properly prepared I mean sealed with a primer or sealer paint when the house was built. Or if a previous owner applied the wallcovering over the painted wall, that's okay. But if the builder took a shortcut and applied wallcovering over the fresh wallboard without the necessary sealer or primer, you could remove the paper coating of the wallboard itself along with the wallcovering, thus exposing the chalky board. The best way to make sure is to do a test strip in a corner behind the door. If the wallboard covering comes off, you have three choices.

1) Let well enough alone and live with your existing wallcovering.

2) Remove all loose paper, sand the seams, and spackle over any imperfections or holes. Then paint over the wallcovering with oil base undercoater. Next paint a finish coat of latex wall paint over your undercoater.

3) Follow the steps in 2) above, but use the first coat of oil paint as a base, and wallpaper over this.

PROCEDURE FOR NORMAL CONDITIONS

First, move the smaller pieces of furniture out of the room. Then move the larger pieces to the center of the room and cover them with a canvas dropcloth or even an old sheet or blanket, but do protect your furniture. Don't use a plastic dropcloth on the floor because it will become slippery when wet. In fact, it is slippery even when dry.

Next, spread newspapers on the floor along the wall. Be generous. Your floor covering should be at least three newspaper sheets thick. The purpose of all this paper, of course, is to absorb the water you'll be using and to catch the wallpaper that will (hopefully) peel off in long wet strips.

Now, check the wallcovering to see if it will come off by pulling at it. If you're lucky, it's vinyl wallcovering and it will simply pull off. But older wallpaper really is paper and to get it off you must wet it with water — thoroughly. If you have a garden-type sprayer, use this for wetting down the wall. If you don't, use a bucket and an old, clean paintbrush and simply "paint" on the water. This is a better technique than using a sponge. You may want to buy a commercial wetting solution to put into the sprayer or bucket.

WARNING: Do not remove the electric switch and outlet plates before you spray or work with water. You can appreciate the hazards of using water-soaked steel wool around exposed wiring.

Soak the wallpaper at least three times. When you can scrape off the paper with your thumbnail it is ready to be removed. A 2½" scraper knife works best; a 3" is also okay, but if your knife is any wider, the scraper blade will ride over hollows in the wall. If the wallpaper dries out or the paper won't come off, apply more water. You want the water to do the work, and usually the more water you use, the easier it is. It's a pleasure when the wallpaper peels off in long strips and a chore if you

start to scrape. Do one wall at a time if you like.

If the wallpaper simply doesn't absorb the water, it has probably been treated with Resistain or some other glaze designed to protect the wallpaper from stains and smudges and to stand up under occasional washings. Also to prevent easy removal. To overcome this problem, you must first sand the paper with a coarse, floor type sandpaper. Scratch the glaze to allow water to get underneath. The commercial wetting agent mentioned earlier will definitely help here.

Remove the Dried Paste

After the wallpaper is removed, you should wash the walls to remove the old wallpaper paste residue. Use hot water in your sprayer (or bucket) to wet down the walls, then rub with coarse steel wool. (A fine grade of steel wool will quickly become clogged with paste and sizing.) It's best to work top to bottom and to concentrate on a small section at a time. Keep the wall wet because the paste should be dissolved by the water, not your rubbing. Don't shortcut this operation because you'll wind up with lumpy walls (ugh!) or worse, a peeling condition with your newly painted walls.

While you are wetting the walls and removing the paper, wash off the baseboard, trim, and woodwork as well. You should also wash the ceiling, especially if there are smokers in the family.

CAUTION: If you have electric baseboard heat, unplug each unit and cover it with plastic to keep the water off.

When all of the paper has been removed and the paste has been washed off, the walls should be smooth and clean. While you are waiting for them to dry, you might clean out your mess of water-soaked newspapers by rolling them up and putting them in a plastic garbage or leaf bag. This is also a good time to cover the floor with a dropcloth to protect it from your painting.

PREPARE THE WALLS

The final step before painting is to fill the cracks and holes in the wall with spackle or plaster. Prepared spackle is good for small cracks and any hole under ⅛″ wide. Anything larger should be filled with plaster. Be sure to include any opening between the walls and the woodwork. Any crack larger than ¼″ should be cut into a V shape before you fill it with plaster. A "church key" can opener is ideal for this. Apply spackle or plaster with a spackle knife. Always wet the crack before plastering (leave dry for spackling) and just mix up a small amount at a time to prevent it drying out.

Holes, nailpops, or loose tape should be filled with wallboard compound. Just follow the directions on the label. There is an additional problem that can occur with wallboard. Contraction or expansion of the walls or the twisting of studs can cause the nails holding the wallboard to pop out. The obvious solution is to drive them back using a sharp blow from a hammer. Then fill in the imprint left by the hammer with spackle or plaster. Or use a punch. (If you're working for a tough boss, you might drive another nail alongside the loose nail to provide added support.)

After all holes and cracks are filled, sand lightly to make the repaired spots as smooth as the rest of the wall. And finally, if all four walls are really smooth, you're ready to prepare the trim.

Assuming that you do intend to paint the trim (don't unless you need to), lightly sand the woodwork to scratch the surface and allow a better bond with the next undercoat. If there are any sags or runs from the previous paint job, sand them off (which is the hard way) or cut them off with a dull chisel knife. To complete the preparation, fill in any holes or gouges with wood paste or putty. Sandpaper smooth and make sure your dust is removed with a duster or tac-cloth. (Or you can use the vacuum.)

One final task — remove the switch plates on the wall and any other fixtures on the woodwork and doors, as well as the window locks and doorknobs. It's easier to remove them than to try to cut around them and wipe off the paint marks later. Now's a good time to clean them, too. As mentioned earlier, if they're brass, drop them in a mixture of vinegar and water and boil for a few minutes. Then dry off and rub with a fine gauge steel wool. They'll look brand new!

NOW TO START THE PAINTING

Start on the ceiling first; top to bottom still applies. You'll need a 9″ roller (we use a medium nap sleeve), a tray for holding the paint, and a 3″ or 2″ brush for cutting around the edges of the ceiling. You also need a stepladder and an extension pole for your roller which will help you to reach the ceiling without climbing up and down the ladder.

Most non-professionals follow the wrong procedure when they cut in around the ceiling with a brush. I'm talking about the strip along the ceiling where it meets the walls. The roller won't fit into the right angle and, while you could do it with a pad, it's generally neater to use a brush. As stated in Chapter 5, you shouldn't cut in the entire side (or even worse, all four sides) because the edges will be dry before your ceiling is painted. If you do, the edges of the ceiling will receive two coats of paint while the center only gets one. The pile-up of paint will often be noticeable, so it's best to follow this method. Start at the narrow edge of the room. Cut in about a two foot strip of the ceiling along the wall. Then roll that area of the ceiling. Cut in another two feet and roll that part of the ceiling. Follow the same procedure for the walls. Painters call this "keeping the edges wet," and it makes for a neater job. Remember also, as it says on the label, "apply liberally."

If you notice that the paint is getting gritty, which could happen before you finish, stop at a logical point, such as the end of a wall, and strain the paint through cheesecloth or pantyhose into a clean bucket. Pantyhose work best. Straining the paint takes but a minute and you'll have a much smoother job with clean paint. Once again, don't stop in the middle of a wall or ceiling.

When you have completed your primer coat on the ceiling and all four walls, you're ready to do the baseboards, door, and woodwork. Many primer coats are specifically formulated for use on both walls and woodwork. We sell one that also dries in two hours so there's little waiting before applying the finish coat. We prefer to use an oil enamel undercoater, but you can use either latex or an oil base.

We also recommend using an oil base enamel finish on the woodwork, but here again, you can also use a latex gloss or semi-gloss.

Before putting on your finish coat, make sure that the primer coat is dry. Scratch it with your fingernail. If you dig into it, wait a day before painting over it. If you paint over wet paint, the second coat could crack.

SUMMARY

■ Determine whether your walls are plaster or wallboard. If wallboard or drywall, read the box at the beginning of the chapter, and proceed with caution.

■ Wet walls thoroughly.

■ Scrape off wallpaper, applying more water if needed.

■ Fill holes with plaster, spackle, or wall compound; sand walls and woodwork; dust clean.

■ Apply primer coat to ceiling and walls; then woodwork.

■ When dry, apply finish coat. Flat for walls, enamel or semi-gloss for woodwork.

7
About Wallcoverings

This chapter on wallcovering is not intended to tell you how to hang wallpaper. See Chapter 8 for the information describing the procedure in detail. You should also carefully read the specific information which can be found in the flyers or instructional literature that come with most rolls of wallpaper.

What I hope to do here is to tell you how to get the walls ready to hang wallcovering and to provide background information that the manufacturer's instructions won't include. Also included are some tips that will help you keep the paper on the wall after you've hung it.

Two improvements have made hanging wallcovering a much easier job — even if you have never attempted it before.

The first is pre-pasted vinyl wallcovering. This is what most homeowners buy. The second is a relatively new acrylic emulsion size that is much more effective than anything available up to now. (We use and sell Wall Prep and Prep Coat. Other brands are called Prep A Wall and Vinyl Prep and there are undoubtedly many other house brands.)

We recommend that you use one of these or a similar product, and follow the instructions on the label.

WALLCOVERING PITFALLS

Even with these two work savers, there are still some things you shouldn't do. Don't:

- Hang paper over raw (untreated) wallboard or drywall
- Paper over latex paint surfaces
- Paper over a glossy surface
- Paper over a poor surface (a wall that is peeling)

When you are making your wallcovering purchase, tell the dealer what you plan to do and ask for advice. But if you are using a pre-pasted wallcovering, make sure that you get an acrylic emulsion size. If for some reason you can't get this product, you can follow the procedure I've used all my life. Before the development of this new product, we routinely painted all walls with an oil base undercoater that dried flat. A glossy paint can't be used because the adhesive might not stick to it.

I've said that you can't paper over raw drywall because it's porous. You must first prime the walls with an oil base undercoater. If you use a latex paint instead of an oil paint, the paper will usually fall off in a matter of months. A chemical reaction takes place between the latex paint and the vinyl paste on the paper which causes the edges of the paper to curl and pull the paint off the wall. This is also true with pre-pasted wallcovering. So the simple solution is an oil base paint that dries flat, or using acrylic emulsion size.

I also mentioned earlier that you can't wallpaper over a surface where the paint is peeling. That's because the covering will stay on only as long as what it's sticking to also stays on. If the paint lets go, the covering will also. You should at least remove as much of the paint as you can before hanging the wallcovering.

Hanging new paper over existing paper is not a good idea either. Yes, it can be done, but your new paper will only be as good as the paste holding the old paper. Putting new on old is not worth it. We suggest that you take the time to remove the old paper and do it right. (See Chapter 6: Painting a Room with Wallpaper for instructions on removing wallpaper.)

If conditions prevent you from removing the old paper and you must apply the new over the old, at least use the acrylic emulsion size we've talked about to increase your chances of having it hold.

If you are going to repaper the wall after you remove the old wallcovering, it isn't necessary to remove all of the old dried paste and residue. Simply sand down the bumps and smooth out the obvious rough spots and hang over it.

However, if you plan to paint over the wall after you have removed the covering, you do have to remove the glue. (See Chapter 6.) Basically you use hot water, rub with steel wool, then rinse. Do a small section at a time.

TYPES OF WALLCOVERING

Most wallcoverings on the market today are vinyl and they're very good quality. You can wash them down, remove spots, and even remove the paper itself (on some types) when you want to put up new. Not too many years ago, when most people used paper wallpaper, there were two specialized wallpaper types that were used in kitchens and bathrooms: Sanitex and Walltex. They were a must for those areas because they were scrubbable. Nowadays, all vinyl papers offer this feature, which is why most of the wallcoverings sold today are vinyl.

Even though you will probably work with a vinyl paper, you might like to know about some of the other kinds of wallcoverings available.

You can still buy the paper-type wallpaper. These are generally the very expensive papers such as hand prints. They're more difficult to handle because most have to be hand trimmed and, being paper, can easily tear when hanging. Older homes probably used this type of paper which should be removed before applying the new.

Lining papers are often used under very expensive papers such as grasscloth and silks which have a rice paper backing. Lining paper is a flat, rather soft, absorbent paper which you apply to your wall with ordinary glue and then hang your good paper on top of this. The lining paper helps to hide any imperfections on the wall and allows the new paper to stick more tightly.

Basically, there are four types of lining papers. One is the conventional fourteen ounce line (a comparatively thin paper) which would be used in the situation just mentioned — as a backing for grasscloth or silk paper. Second, is what is called a "wallcover"; a much heavier paper, made to bridge cracks and joints in the wall. When applied, it becomes rigid enough to bridge the grooves in a brick wall and have the finished wallpaper look reasonably smooth. It will even cover cracks such as you'll find in a cinderblock or cement block wall. It's a specialized paper for a specialized need and it does an excellent job, however wallcover is rather expensive.

The third type of lining paper is much like the fourteen ounce conventional paper except that it's pre-pasted and scrubbable. The fourth type is similar except that it's strippable — you can remove it easily when you want to.

Unless a wallpaper is truly a paper, it is usually referred to as a wallcovering. When you read the labels or look through the wallcovering books, you will observe that you now have a number of options or special features such as pre-pasted, stain resistant, washable or scrubbable, and dry strippable (it comes off easily). Even so, please read the instructions carefully, and make certain that the wall is prepped for hanging.

SUMMARY

■ Remove existing wallpaper. (See Chapter 6.)

■ Prep wall if necessary.

■ Use an acrylic emulsion size for hanging the wallcovering.

■ If you are using a special paper, consider the use of a lining paper.

8
How to Hang Wallcoverings

EQUIPMENT NEEDED

- ☐ Stepladder
- ☐ Wallpaper table
- ☐ Water box
- ☐ Carpenter's level
- ☐ Sponge
- ☐ Plumb bob
- ☐ Smoothing brush
- ☐ Spackle knife
- ☐ Razor knife
- ☐ Scissors
- ☐ Seam roller/corner roller
- ☐ Size

Some of this equipment may be unfamiliar, so here are short descriptions of the more specialized items.

The wallpaper table is three feet wide and six feet long. It's usually made of light half inch wood, but you can use a sheet of cut-down plywood (which usually comes in a 4′ × 8′ sheet) or a flush door. The table is usually supported by two trestles. Professional trestles can be height adjusted; most use a waist-high setting. You can use ordinary saw-horses, but you'll have to do more bending over which might become tiresome.

The water box is a plastic container, approximately 32″ long, 7″ wide, and about 4″ deep. It resembles a window box planter. Don't fill it more than ¾ full.

A carpenter's level is about three feet long with small, liquid-filled glass tubes. You center the air bubble in the tube to get a straight line or to determine if the surface is true.

A plumb bob is a string with a small pointed weight at one end and is used to make a perfect vertical line.

The smoothing brush or sweep is used to flatten the wallpaper on the wall. It has a flat wood back (to hold the bristles), measures twelve to fourteen inches long, and has a half inch thick handle. The bristles can be nylon or natural bristle and can vary from ¾″ long (for vinyl) to about 2″ (for light-weight paper covering). The longer the bristle, the

Necessary (& Optional) Wallpaper Tools & Materials

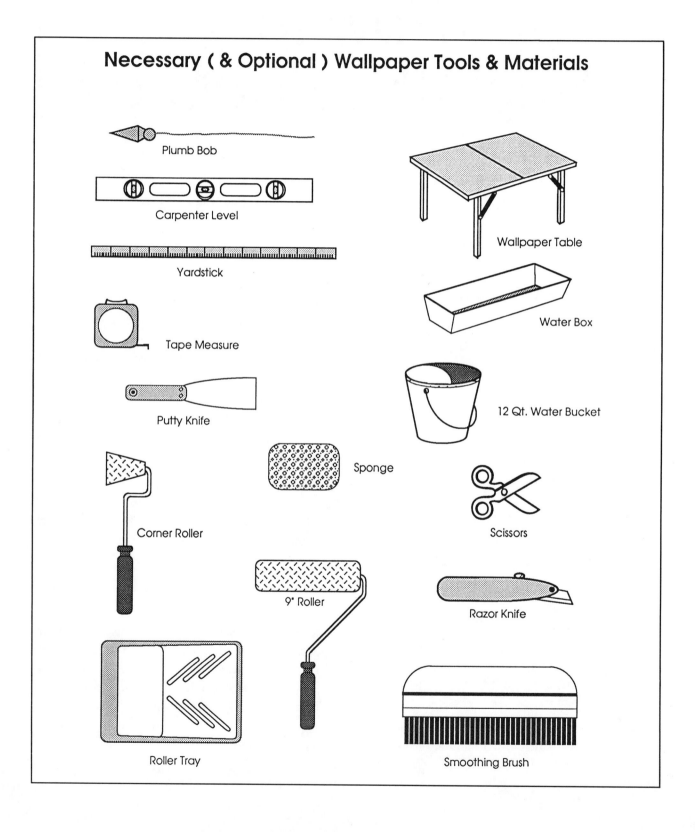

Plumb Bob

Carpenter Level

Yardstick

Tape Measure

Putty Knife

Corner Roller

Sponge

9" Roller

Roller Tray

Wallpaper Table

Water Box

12 Qt. Water Bucket

Scissors

Razor Knife

Smoothing Brush

softer it is. You need the longer sweep for lighter weight covering.

The razor blade holder is best for cutting wallcovering, but scissors will come in handy.

A seam roller is used to make certain that the wallcovering seams (where the two strips abut) are firmly and smoothly affixed to the wall. It is a hard plastic roller attached to a handle. A corner roller does the same job in the corner of the wall where the seam roller can't reach. This is a shaped roller, wide in the middle, narrow at the ends to fit in the wall corner.

NOTE: If you use pre-pasted covering you won't need the following paste tools.

There is a special paste brush for applying paste to the wallcovering, but we use a six inch paintbrush and you can also use a four inch brush. Better yet, use a seven inch short nap roller for applying most kinds of paste.

Size is a liquid wall preparation which is used to 1) seal the wall, and 2) make it easier to position the soaked wallcovering strips on the wall.

MEASURING YOUR ROOM

This is usually step one. Before you can buy your wallcovering you must know how many rolls to buy. When you do buy, keep these three rules in mind.

1. Buy more than you need.

2. Don't buy a lot more than you need.

3. Don't buy a lot more unless you choose a large repeat pattern. (More about patterns later.)

There are two ways to determine how much wallcovering you need. You can figure it out yourself or you can let the wallcovering store clerk do it . . . after you have supplied the basic size of your room. Most of our customers prefer to let us do the figuring.

The easy way to buy wallcovering is to let the owner or assistant at your wallcovering store do it for you when you provide him or her with the following basic information. Measure the length of your room, the width of the room, and the height of the ceiling. Count the number of doors and windows and write down all this information. Then, while you are picking out the pattern, the wallcovering specialist will figure out the number of rolls you will need, depending on the wallcovering you choose.

Virtually any paint store that sells wallcovering or any wallcovering specialty store should be willing and able to provide this service; wallcovering departments in mass merchandising stores might or might not.

How do you figure out how much wallcovering to buy? Let's say that you are planning to cover a bedroom which measures 9' × 12' with an 8' ceiling (the walls are 8' high). Since wallcovering comes in square foot rolls, you must find out how many square feet make up your four walls.

The formula is length or width x height (in feet) equals square feet.

One wall is 9' wide × 8' high which equals 72 square feet. You have two of these walls (72 square feet × 2) which equals 144 square feet. The other wall is 12' long × 8' high which equals 96 square feet. You have two of these walls (96 square feet × 2) which equals 192 square feet. The total of all four walls (144 + 192 = 336) is 336 square feet.

Deducting Doors and Windows

Measure the square feet of the two doors (one is a closet, the other your entry into the room) and deduct the door total from your wall total. Say your doors measure 3' × 7' or 21 square feet × 2 doors = 42 square feet.

You have two windows. A typical window measures 30″ wide (including the window frames) and 60″ high (also including the frames).

For our example, let's use a measurement of 24″ high instead of 30″ and call it 2′ wide by 60″ or 5′ high. (We're deducting less to give us a slight safety factor.) Thus 2′ × 5′ = 10 square feet. Multiplied by two windows this gives a window total of 20 square feet. This gives us a total deduction of 62 square feet (42 square feet of doors, plus 20 square feet of windows). So 336 square feet of wall space, less 62 square feet of doors and windows leaves 274 square feet to be covered.

If you are buying a covering sold in the American Single Roll which contains 36 square feet per roll, you would need 7.6 rolls (274 square feet divided by 36). So you should buy eight rolls plus an additional roll for safety's sake, or a total of nine rolls.

NOTE: It's always best to have additional paper to correct any possible mistakes.

ADDITIONAL FACTORS

There are two other considerations you should keep in mind before buying wallcoverings.

Types of Rolls

The covering you select could be put up in any of these three types of rolls:

American Single Roll — contains 36 square feet

Euro or European Single — contains 28 square feet

Metric Single — contains 20 square feet

The wallcovering you select, whether it's from a book or stock, should tell you the type of roll it comes on and the number of square feet each roll contains.

Thus, if the paper you selected came on a Metric Single Roll, you would need about fifteen rolls using the sample room measurements above.

Prices vary as well. Comparing two, equal in quality wallcoverings, the price per roll of an American Single Roll should be considerably higher than a Metric Single Roll, because the first contains almost twice as much paper as the second.

REMINDER: Read the instructions that come with the wallcovering you purchase.

TYPES OF WALLCOVERING

Almost all wallcoverings today are pre-pasted. But some of the more expensive coverings such as grasscloth, silk, and hand-blocked paper are not. (Many of these are not trimmed either.) And, while pre-pasted coverings are easier to hang, especially for the first-time user, the basic application procedures are the same for both pre-pasted and non-pasted. Special instructions for the latter are included later in the chapter.

Each type of covering comes with or requires its own paste or adhesive for best results. Get all the information you can from the salesperson and before you start, read the instructions carefully.

Regular paper — wheat or cellulose paste

Lightweight, pre-pasted, paper-backed vinyl — adhesive on back

Lightweight, non-pasted vinyl — powdered vinyl adhesive

Cloth-backed vinyl or vinyl fabric — pre-mixed adhesive

Heavy cloth-backed vinyl — pre-mixed adhesive

Heavy paper-backed vinyl — pre-mixed adhesive

PREPARING THE WALLS

If you consider buying the wallcovering step one, then this is step two. It's not just important. It is imperative! Virtually all walls need some preparation. The wall that you intend to cover probably falls into one of the following categories.

Existing Wallcovering

Procedure: Remove the existing wallcovering. (See Chapter 5 for detailed instructions about how best to do this.) After the paper has been removed, sand down the old dried paste and residue. It isn't necessary to prepare the wall as completely as if you were planning to paint, but you should sand over the bumps and obvious rough spots. The wall should be dry before hanging new paper.

Alternate procedure: It is best to remove the existing wallcovering but, if you don't want to bother with the mess of removal, you can paper over existing wallcovering . . . with certain reservations. You must remove all loose wallcovering. If most of the wallcovering is tight, glue the loose edges and wash the walls to remove any grease. Then size the wall and apply your new covering.

You should not put new wallcovering over metallic, embossed, foil, or flocked paper. These must be removed first. It's really best to remove all existing paper, otherwise your new covering is only as good as the paste that's holding up your existing paper. Generally, your investment in new wallcovering is such that it's worth your effort to do it right and get a longer lasting job.

Previously Painted Walls

Procedure: For flat paint — Wash the walls with detergent to remove dirt and grease. Scrape off any loose paint, fill in any cracks with spackle, and sand smooth. Size the wall with an acrylic emulsion and start with your wallcovering.

For glossy paint — Wash the walls with detergent, scrape off loose paint, fill in any cracks, and sand lightly. Brush off the dust. Size walls with acrylic emulsion and apply wallcovering.

New or Unpainted Walls

You can't paper over raw plaster or drywall because the wall is porous. First prime the wall with an oil base primer paint. Then size the walls and start to cover. (You can also use a latex primer but you then must use an acrylic size.)

CHECKLIST

Before hanging your covering, run through this list to make certain that you are ready.

☐ You have your wallcovering on hand — enough rolls to cover and extra for errors.

☐ You have prepped the walls. (See pages 61-62 and/or Chapter 5.)

☐ You have the necessary tools. (See opening of this chapter.)

☐ Furniture is moved out of the room or away from the walls.

☐ Switch plates have been removed. The best idea is to turn off the electricity in the room that you're working on — an absolute must if you are using metallic paper. (This means, of course, that you won't be able to work at night.)

☐ Check your run numbers. Make sure the rolls have the same dye lot number, otherwise there could be a difference in color.

☐ Read carefully the instructions enclosed in the roll of wallcovering.

For the purposes of this discussion, I am going to assume that your covering is pre-pasted. It's best to start with this because it's easier to hang and easier to explain. We'll discuss paste-it-yourself wallcovering later.

One handy trick we use is to get a card table and

place it at the head of your wallpaper table. It should be three or four inches lower than the work table. Then put the water box on the card table. This is so that after you soak your rolled-up wallcovering, you can pull the strip up on your wallpaper table. It's not essential, but does make it a lot easier to handle the strips.

HANGING PRE-PASTED WALLCOVERING

Before you start measuring, you should know that your walls and ceiling are probably not exactly true, but that your covering is true, so you'll have to make slight adjustments. You make these adjustments at each corner of the room.

First, measure the width of your covering; say it's 20½" wide. Next, start in the corner farthest from you as you come in the door and measure out ½" less than the width of the covering, i.e., 20". (That half inch will be wrapped around the corner of the wall that abuts the wall you're starting on.) Then, using your level or a plumb line (20" out from the corner) make a straight vertical line with a pencil from the ceiling to the top of the baseboard. (We find it easier to use a regular carpenter's level than a plumb bob to get a straight vertical line, but you can use either.) Measure the height of that line, then add four to six inches to that measurement. This is to allow a couple of inches at both the top and bottom of your strip so your cut fits tight against the ceiling and baseboard.

Now make your first cut of wallcovering. Roll the strip backwards loosely, paste side out, and put it in the water box for about thirty seconds. Hold the paper by the end and pull it out of the water onto the table — design side facing the table — making sure that all of the paste on the back of the covering is wet. Fold your strip halfway to the middle lightly (glue to glue), then pull out the rest and fold the bottom half to the middle. Fold lightly, and overlap your bottom fold about a half inch. Make sure that the edges line up and smooth out any wrinkles

or bubbles with your hand. Now roll up the paper loosely (still folded), and let it relax in the water three or four minutes before hanging. Don't make creases. Follow the instructions that come with your covering. Depending on the thickness of the covering, the instructions might say to allow three, four, or five minutes for soaking. You should not, however, let the paper soak too long or the paste will dissolve.

Next, remove the wallcovering from the water box. Unfold the top part and, holding the strip on either side at the top, lay it flush with your line. (You'll probably have to climb your stepladder to do this.) Then, pick up the strip and unfold the top part to hang on the wall, leaving the bottom part still folded until the top is properly aligned. Now reach down and pull down the bottom fold which will drop into place.

Overlap the ceiling about two inches and position your strip, top to bottom, flush against your pencil line. You can slide the strip left or right, up or down to adjust. (Sizing on the wall helps the strip slide.) Then, with your smoothing brush, sweep your strip down the wall and you'll automatically overlap the next wall by a half inch. (You will need this overlap when you finish each corner, in the meantime, just leave it. You might slit it at the top and bottom so it fits snugly.) With your spackle knife, push the covering firmly into the corner where the wall meets the ceiling. Don't cut the covering but make sure it fits tight. Then, with your knife firmly against the ceiling, hold your razor knife in your other hand and cut the covering across the full width of your spackle knife. Then move your spackle knife over and make another cut the width of your blade. Continue until the entire strip along the ceiling is cut, including the half inch overlap on the adjoining wall. Cutting against your spackle knife helps ensure a straight edge at the ceilng.

Now peel off the strip on the ceiling and wash off the paste on the ceiling. (Paste turns brown when it dries.) Use the same technique to cut along the

Add about 6" to room height measurement and cut strip. Roll backwards (pattern in) for soaking.

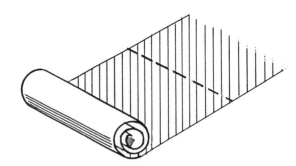

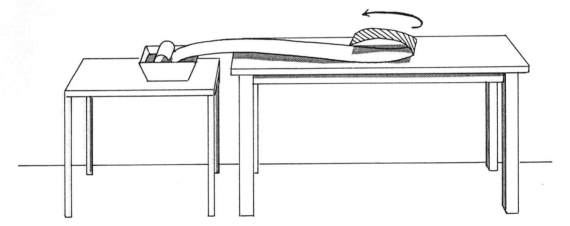

Use a card table at a lower height to hold the water box. Pull the cut strip up on the table and fold — glue side to glue side.

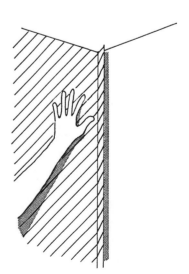

Mark the vertical line ½" less than the width of the paper so you can overlap the adjoining wall.

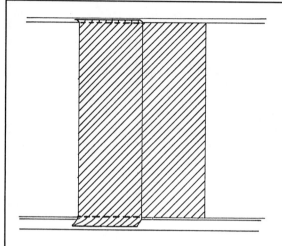

Butt strips and match patterns but don't overlap. Do overlap the ceiling and baseboard.

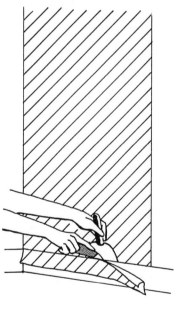

Cut off excess using spackle knife and clean razor blade. Change razor blades every few strips for clean cuts.

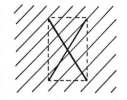

Turn off electricity when hanging wallcovering and remove outlet plates. Cut an "X", then the outline. The plate will cover the cut edges.

top of the baseboard, then wash the paste off the baseboard. Finally, using your sponge, wash off any paste on the face of your paper. Then use your corner roller to make sure your strip fits snugly.

The trick to cutting is to keep your razor blade clean and to change blades as often as you need. When paste collects and hardens on the blade it causes the paper edge to tear rather than cut.

Before you cut your second strip, hold the cut end of the roll at the ceiling (roll on the floor) and match your pattern. Then make sure you have a sufficient overlap at the ceiling and baseboard and make your cut. Repeat your actions for hanging the second strip. (These are: Roll up lightly [backwards, glue side out] and soak for thirty seconds. Pull the paper up on your work table and fold, top to middle, bottom to middle [glue to glue], roll lightly, and soak. Hang the strip, top to bottom, overlapping the ceiling and baseboard. Sweep smooth, cut off ceiling and baseboard overlap, wash off the paste; then cut and hang the next strip.)

When you hang your second strip, don't overlap the first. Just butt this strip tightly against the first, making sure that the patterns match exactly. After your two strips have been up for about ten minutes, run a seam roller along the seam to make certain it's tightly pasted and won't pull off later. Do this with each seam.

Once you get into the swing of things you can take shortcuts like cutting a couple of strips so that the second can be soaking while you're hanging and trimming the first. But don't get carried away and cut too many strips because you will soon run into obstacles which might call for a different set of measurements. Your first obstacle could be a window. This might sound formidable, but it actually takes longer to explain the procedure than to do it. And once you've done it, the next one is easy.

NOTE: These instructions are more difficult to explain than to perform. Read them aloud or go over them several times to help you visualize the steps outlined.

MEASURING FOR A WINDOW

The last strip that you hang before coming to a window will probably not fit snugly up against the window frame. For example, suppose there is a 10″ space between the edge of your pasted strip and the window frame. Here is the technique to use.

Cut a full width strip from your roll the same height as your first strip. Roll it lightly (backwards) and soak for thirty seconds. Then pull it up onto your work table and fold it top to middle, bottom to middle (glue side to glue side). The eight foot-plus strip is now four feet (plus overlap). This makes it much easier to handle. Measure off eleven inches wide and cut a vertical strip with your cutting knife through both thicknesses. Use a metal straight edge to make sure the cut is true. (The additional inch of width will be for the overlap.) Roll up the strip and soak again. (Follow instructions for soaking.) Then hang this eleven inch wide strip, overlapping the window frame. Sweep as before, and make your overlap cuts at the top, bottom, and side.

You still have a piece approximately half as wide as your regular strips. Use matching parts of this for the header and the footer, which is what we call the wall spaces over and under the window.

Measure the height from over the window frame to the ceiling. Add five or six inches for overlap and make your cut across the strip. (Make sure your pattern matches before you cut.) Measure the space under the window frame and do the same. Soak and hang. You now have part of your header and footer covered. Follow the same procedure for the remainder of the window. Measure the width of the uncovered header and footer, then make your vertical cut. However, since the average window (the outside frame) is about thirty-two inches, you might have to make three header cuts, depending on the width of your initial strip.

When you hang the second vertical at the other side of the window frame, don't overlap the frame because you won't be able to match the patterns at the top and bottom of the window.

Other obstacles might be an electrical outlet plug or a switch plate. Before hanging your strip, make sure that the plates have been removed and the electricity in that room turned off. Then cover over these outlet openings but mark where they are. Make an "X" cut over the opening with your razor and remove the excess. Turning the power off is a necessary safety precaution because you will be cutting near exposed wires with a metal knife. After the excess wallcovering has been removed, put the plate back on to hold the edges in place until dry.

ADJUSTING THE CORNERS

When you reach your first corner, the procedure is slightly different. If you don't have the space for a full width strip, cut to fit as you did with the window. Measure the width of the space and add a half inch for the overlap. Then make your vertical cut to fit. Use the rest of your strip for the return wall. But before you hang, you must realign. Measure the width of your strip and with your level or plumb line make a pencil line, as you did initially, from ceiling to baseboard. Position your strip along your pencilled line and overlap that half inch strip into the corner. This is where you make your adjustment. If the wall corner is not exactly true (and it probably isn't), you might have ¼″ at the top and the full ½″ at the bottom. You must do this at each corner. There will be a slight mismatch in the corner but this will be far less noticeable than a crooked hang.

Another handy tip: Some of the lightweight prepasted vinyls and all of the heavy vinyls require a special adhesive when you overlap. Ask about this

when you buy your covering. We use one called Stanfix that comes in a squeeze tube. (It allows vinyl to stick to vinyl.) Run a bead of this adhesive down the corner on top of the overlapped piece.

Follow this procedure in each corner until you get back to the door where you came in. You started at the farthest corner so if there were any mismatches, this will be the least noticeable part of the wall.

ADDITIONAL OBSTACLES

While switchplates are relatively easy, the thermostat might be a little more troublesome. Most are screwed onto the wall. The cover is often screwed or fitted onto a plate which is screwed to the wall. It's usually best to remove the cover and carefully cut the paper to fit around the plate. If you were to remove the plate and unhook the wires, they could fall back into the wall. It's a devil of a job to fish them out.

Heat registers are treated like electrical outlet plates. Remove the cover, paper over the space, cut around the hole, and put the cover back.

Radiators, which are common in older homes, are the most difficult. If it is the steam register type and you are working during warm weather, you might want to unhook it at the single pipe and move it out of the way. If it's a hot water radiator, don't touch it. But do be sure to turn off any radiator if you're working around it.

Most radiators are placed under windows and sit about two inches out from the wall — not leaving enough room to work behind. We usually measure the space and allow a two inch overlap at the top and bottom. Then slowly slide the strip in behind the radiator, using a smoothing brush or even a yardstick. Sometimes a small towel fitted over a yardstick can smooth out the strip.

We use a special trimming knife with a long handle which is worth buying if you have radiators. Or you can tape your cutting knife on the yardstick to cut the overlap. If all else fails, slide the paper out, cut to fit exactly and slide it back in. Many homeowners find this last technique easiest. Even if there is a slight mismatch no one will know but you.

Cabinets

Kitchens and baths almost always contain cabinets or medicine cabinets that you must wallpaper around. Measure from the last strip hung to the cabinet at the top, middle, and bottom of the cabinet. Take the widest measurement and add one inch. Mark this measurement on the new strip of wallpaper starting from the matching side of the strip. Cut the strip in two, using scissors or a sharp razor blade. Wet the strip as the instructions indicate, match it to the strip on the wall and smooth down. The other side of the strip will overlap the cabinet. Clip into the overlap at the corners, and trim the excess away along the cabinet only.

For the remaining half of the strip, measure the distance from the ceiling to the top of the cabinet. Cut the top part 1″ longer (plus your overlap onto the celing for trimming) from the remaining piece. The best way to do this is to hold the piece up and match it, then cut it slightly longer than where the match hits the top of the cabinet. Follow the same procedure underneath the cabinet, working with the bottom of the strip. Wet the two remaining pieces, match, and hang. Trim away the overlaps. Continue to hang over the top and under the bottom of the cabinets with short pieces that match.

Ceilings

If you plan to wallpaper a ceiling, do so before you do the walls. It is easier to hang strips running the width of the room as it is shorter, but consider the whole room when deciding which direction to go. Mark your guideline on the ceiling just as described for the walls. Follow the wetting instructions included by the manufacturer. Align the first strip with your line. Have your partner hold the rest of the strip for you as you position it and smooth it down. If you're also going the cover the walls, trim the ceilng paper so there is a ¼″ overlap onto the walls. If you're hanging the ceiling only, trim the excess with your razor and spackling knife.

Rectangular Archways

When papering a room with a rectangular archway, always do that wall first. The first strip should fall so that enough of the righthand side of the strip overlaps the arch itself to cover it. A horizontal cut will be made precisely at the top edge of the arch over to the wall. The wallcovering below the cut will wrap around the lefthand vertical of the arch.

Next, cut three short strips long enough to wrap around the underside of the arch. The next long strip on the right side of the arch should be wide enough on the left side to wrap around the arch. Again, you will make a horizontal cut at the top of the arch.

After hanging these strips, fill in the area on the underside of the arch at the left and right corners. Cut matching pieces. Tuck the upper ends under the wallcovering on the face of the arch, and smooth the pieces onto the underside of the arch, filling the space.

Curved Archways

Wallpapering a curved arch is similar to the rectangular arch except that a separate piece is used to cover the inside of the arch. You should have at least two inches extra to wrap to the inside of the arch. Hang the strips around and above the arch as usual, letting the excess hang free in the archway. Cut away the excess, but leave two inches to wrap to the inside. In the curve of the arch, cut small wedge-shaped clips almost to the edge. Wrap the wallcovering to the inside of the arch and smooth down.

To cover the archway itself, figure the pattern match from the bottom up. Cut two pieces ½″ less than the width of the arch and long enough to cover from the middle of the arch down each side. Hang the strips from the center down the sides with the edge of the wallcovering ¼″ from the edge of the archway. If you're using vinyl wallcovering, be sure to use vinyl-to-vinyl adhesive for the overlap.

HELPFUL HINTS

Patterns

Suppose the pattern you chose features rows of alternating red and yellow apples running horizontally across the walls. There is a space of six inches between each row. The repeat of the pattern would be considered six inches, and there would be very little waste paper between your cuts. Contrast this with a pattern of apple trees with a space of two feet between the horizontal rows of trees. When matching here, your waste could be as much as two feet and this will affect your safety factor when ordering.

Soaking

Make sure you allow your wallcovering to soak or relax before hanging. Wallcovering will swell slightly after it's pasted. Soaking allows the swelling to take place in the water box before you get it up on the wall.

If you get vertical blisters after the strip is hung it usually means that the paper didn't soak long enough.

As you're hanging, if the covering won't slide easily, the paper is probably too dry. Re-soak and try again. If it still won't slide, the wall has not been properly sized and it's too porous. Your paste is soaking into the wall and drying out the paper. If

the seams are shrinking, it could be caused by insufficient soaking.

Textured Wallcovering

Textures, weaves, grasscloths, and silks are generally random match coverings. They are sometimes slightly shaded, that is, the color can vary from one side of the strip to the other. It's best to reverse every other strip when hanging these random match coverings. You'll find the shading looks better when you hang every other piece upside down.

Miscellaneous Tips

■ When hanging a large scale pattern in a room with a fireplace, center the first strip over the fireplace and hang in a righthand direction to the corner. Then go back to the center and hang to the left corner.

■ Never wrap a whole strip around inside corners without cutting and lining it up again. It may look fine at first, but within a few weeks creases and wrinkles may appear.

■ Never use a seam roller on flocked wallcovering. Instead, tap the seams gently with your smoothing brush.

■ If you don't plan to paper into the inside of an arch or frameless window or door, trim the wallcovering with your razor blade ¼″ from the outer edge. This prevents fraying or pulling from the outside edge.

■ If you're wallpapering a ceiling, plan to end up in an inconspicuous part of the room such as above the entrance.

NON-PASTED WALLCOVERING

As stated earlier, most wallcovering is now prepasted, but if you fall in love with a silk or hand-blocked print, it may be the non-pasted type. Past-ing yourself is a bit more difficult, but the technique is the same. This is the procedure we use.

Cut the strip to size as previously explained. Lay this strip on the wallpaper table design side down. Then apply the manufacturer's recommended paste. It is most important that you use the right paste.

Applying paste can be tricky because you must put paste on the entire back of the strip, especially the edges. However, in doing this, you cannot slop over on the table because you might then get paste on the front, or design side, of the covering. And if you do, it is difficult to get it off the visible side of your covering. Unfortunately, if you protect yourself by not quite reaching the edge, the covering won't stick to the wall. So we do this.

Place three cut strips face down on the wallpaper table, and arrange them so that each strip overlaps the other. (As if you were playing cards and showing a partner your hand.) Place the top strip along the front edge of the table and apply paste. The opposite side of the top strip overlaps the strip below. When you put paste on this edge it will slop over on the back of the sheet below and will keep the table clean.

When the entire back side is covered with paste, fold one end up to the middle. Keep paste side to paste side. Then turn the other end to the middle but don't overlap because you'll get paste on the front.

Pick up the strip and unfold the top part to hang on the wall, leaving the bottom part still folded until the top is properly aligned. Then reach down and pull down the bottom fold which will drop into place. (This is the same procedure as for hanging pre-pasted wallcovering.)

You can use a brush or a seven inch short nap roller to apply the paste. We prefer the roller.

SUMMARY

■ Before purchasing wallcovering, measure the room. Measure length, width, and height of walls; count doors and windows. Then let the dealer at the wallcovering store compute the number of rolls needed.

■ There are three types of rolls; each contains a different amount of square footage of paper. Read carefully.

■ Most people buy pre-pasted vinyl wallcovering; it's the easiest to hang.

Existing Wallcovering

■ Remove old paper before recovering for best results.

Previously Painted Walls

■ Prepare walls, size with acrylic emulsion, and hang new paper.

New or Unpainted Walls

■ Don't hang over raw plaster or drywall. Prime wall first with oil base primer.

Hanging Pre-pasted Wallcovering

■ Read the step-by-step instructions on pages 70 to 73. Try to visualize the steps as you read them aloud BEFORE you start to hang the wallcovering.

9
Staining

EQUIPMENT NEEDED

☐ Brush(es) for staining and varnishing

☐ Clean rags

☐ Sandpaper

☐ Stirring stick

☐ Plastic gloves

☐ Hammer and nail set

☐ Colored putty

☐ Work bucket (especially for exterior)

INTERIOR STAINING

Staining Trim in a New Room

The proper procedure is to stain and varnish your woodwork before painting the walls and ceiling. Stain is best applied with a bristle brush and the excess wiped off lightly with a clean rag after it has a chance to penetrate (read directions on the label). After the stain has been applied and dried, run your hand or a clean cloth across the stained area.

If the stain has raised the grain and it feels rough to your hand or cloth, you should sand lightly and dust. Next (if one coat of stain is sufficient), you should brush on a coat of polyurethane or varnish before you start to paint the walls and ceiling. This is to protect the newly stained surface from paint spills and spatters. You can apply the final polyurethane coat after painting.

Following is the procedure, from the top, one step at a time, through sand, seal, stain, and finish on new, untreated wood.

Let's assume that you have already sanded the surface smooth and dusted off the residue. Next — maybe — you should seal the wood. If the carpenter has used the same grade of wood throughout, and if it's a hardwood, you probably won't have to seal. But, if you are staining a soft wood such as pine, or if you have several different grades of the same wood or different kinds of wood, or if you're staining plywood (which has a "wild" grain), then it's best to use a sealer before the stain.

As you will note when you check out your stains at the paint store, most labels state that you don't have to use a sealer or conditioner before applying the stain. But many stain manufacturers also put out a sealer or wood conditioner whose label says you should use a sealer, especially on a soft wood such as pine.

The labels also say that you don't have to sand after using the stain. And often you don't. But let your own sense of touch be the judge, and certainly don't make additional work for yourself if you don't have to.

On our staining jobs we now seal wood the easy way with an excellent product called Wood Conditioner made by the Minwax Company. Just follow the directions on the label. (The hard way, which I've done most of my painting career, is to apply a coat of shellac, cut way back with alcohol, to the raw wood before applying the stain.)

Getting the Right Shade of Stain

All labels advise you to "experiment" before applying stain on your woodwork. It's essential that you do, but it's also a Catch-22. How can you test unless you buy the stain, and why should you buy the stain unless you're sure it's what you want?

The best procedure is to consult the chip chart that most stain manufacturers display. Decide which stain sample is most like the finish you'd like to achieve on your trim. Then buy the smallest can available and experiment with samples of the same kind of wood used in your woodwork. Apply one coat, then another sample with two coats and also apply a coat of polyurethane or varnish. Each coat will make it slightly darker. If it's still not exactly right, buy another stain or mix two stains together and experiment again using one and two coats.

If the stain you've bought is too dark, a neutral stain mixed with it will lighten the shade. While you're in the testing stage, buy the smallest possible containers until you have your exact formula. If you are using a paint store, the owner or manager will probably help you reduce the trial and error time and cost.

Applying and Finishing

We have found that stain is best applied with a bristle brush (if it's oil based) and a smaller, rather than larger brush (because it's so thin it runs all over). Some people like to use a rag to apply stain. This is effective but it is messier and it uses much more stain. If you decide to use a rag, consider wearing disposable plastic gloves to keep the stain from under your fingernails.

After the stain has been applied and has dried, you should fill the nail holes. Make sure all of the nails are set (hammered in slightly below the surface of the wood). If they are not, use a nail set and drive in each nail to the proper depth. Your paint store sells little jars of colored putty. There is a wide selection of colors so you can easily match your stain. Press a small ball of putty over each nail hole and cut it off with your putty knife.

Often the putty is too thin to use properly and it handles like chocolate icing. You can easily thicken it with plaster of paris or even flour. If it becomes too dry, add a little mineral spirits.

If the grain has been raised by your stain, sand lightly and dust before applying a coat of polyurethane or varnish before beginning to paint your walls and ceiling. This will protect your stain from paint spatters or spills. The final coat of polyurethane or varnish should be applied after your walls and ceiling are done. Sand lightly and dust before putting on the final coat. If you feel up to it, two coats are better than one, but remember to sand lightly and dust between coats.

NOTE ON FLOORS: If you or your carpenter have laid down a new hardwood floor, this should be finished last, after the trim has been stained and the walls and ceiling have been painted. The final sanding of the floor will take care of any paint spills before the floor finish is applied.

If you plan to carpet, you will probably have a subflooring such as a chipboard, which is okay as is.

EXTERIOR STAINING

There are many different kinds of stains, so we won't attempt to cover them all. Oil stain is far more widely used than latex stain. Exterior stains are usually categorized as solid covering, semi-solid, or transparent stains. The names are misleading because semi-solid stains are anything but. They're thin and penetrate any porous surface, which is the primary purpose of using them. The oil penetration provides excellent protection. Solid covering stains are much like thin paint and can even be applied over a painted surface to "even out" a house. For example, if your house is stained and your garage door has been painted (and it sticks out like a sore thumb), you can use a solid cover stain over the paint and make the door look like the rest of the house.

However, the most common use of stain is on a wood surface where the owner wants to preserve the "wood" look. This could be cedar or redwood siding, shingles, or virtually any wood used for decking, fences, or any other kind of home construction. Stains come in a great variety of colors, often named after wood finishes. There is usually no problem about finding the exterior shade you want.

A water-repellent preservative may be used as a natural finish. It reduces warping, prevents staining at the edges and ends of wood siding, and helps control mildew growth. Water-repellent preservatives contain a fungicide, a small amount of wax as a water repellant, a resin or drying oil, and a solvent such as turpentine or mineral spirits. Water-repellent preservatives do not contain any coloring pigments but will darken the color of the wood.

The initial application of a water-repellent preservative to a smooth surface is short lived, usually one to two years on smooth surfaces and one to three years on roughsawn surfaces. During the first few years, a fresh finish may have to be applied every year or two. But after the wood has gradually weathered to a uniform tan color, additional treatments may last two to four years because the weathered boards absorb more of the finish.

CAUTION: Water-repellent preservatives should always be mixed and applied very carefully. The safest place for mixing is outdoors. Solutions with solvents are volatile and flammable. Wear protective clothing on hands and arms and take care not to splash the solution into eyes or on the face.

To apply water-repellent preservatives, liberally brush the solutions onto all lap and butt joints, edges and ends of boards, and edges of panels where end grain occurs. Don't overlook other areas especially vulnerable to moisture such as the bottoms of doors and window frames. One gallon will usually cover about 250 square feet of smooth surface or 100 to 150 square feet of rough surface.

Semi-transparent penetrating stains are water-repellent preservatives or water repellants with a small amount of pigment. The pigment particles help protect the wood surface from the effects of sunlight. These stains penetrate the wood surface to a degree and will not trap moisture that encourages decay. They will not blister or peel even if moisture gets into the wood. Penetrating stains are oil- or alkyd-based, and some may contain a fungicide or water repellant. Latex-based stains are also available, but they do not penetrate the wood surface as the oil-based stains do.

Semi-transparent penetrating stains are most effective on rough lumber surfaces. They are available in a variety of colors and are especially popular in the brown or red earth tones. They will not work over a solid-color stain or old coat of paint.

The first application of a semi-transparent penetrating stain should last about two or three years. When refinished after weathering, the finish will usually last much longer. Two coats of stain applied to the weathered surface may last eight years or more.

Semi-transparent penetrating stains may be brushed, sprayed, or rolled on, with brushing giving the best penetration and performance. Lap marks will form if the front edge of the stained area dries out before a logical stopping place is reached. Apply the stain to a small number of boards or a single panel at a time to avoid lap marks.

One gallon of semi-transparent penetrating stain will usually cover about 200 to 400 square feet of smooth surface and 100 to 200 square of rough or weathered surface. For the longest life, use two coats and apply the second coat before the first is dry. (If the first coat dries completely, the second coat will not be able to penetrate the wood.) About an hour after applying the second coat, use a cloth, sponge, or dry brush, lightly wetted with stain, to wipe off the excess stain that has not penetrated the wood. If you don't do this, the wood will form an unsightly surface film and glossy spots.

Latex semitransparent stains do not penetrate the wood surface but are easy to apply and less likely to form lap marks. For a long life, two coats, applying the second coat any time after the first has dried, should be used. The second coat will remain free of gloss even on smooth wood. These stains are essentially very thin paints and will perform accordingly.

CAUTION: Sponges or cloths that are wet with oil-based stain are particularly susceptible to spontaneous combustion. To prevent fires, immerse them in water or seal them in an airtight container immediately after use.

Solid stains can, but semi-solid and semi-transparent stains cannot, be used over a painted area or over a sealed wood area. This might sound like heresy coming from a painter, but in my opinion, stain is the only way to go. If I were building a new house, I would stain it, not paint it, because you get so much more for your money with stain. It never peels and you only need to restain about every five or six years; maybe four or five years on the sunny side.

When you buy stain for exterior work (probably in gallon cans), you should handle it much like paint. Make sure that it's thoroughly stirred at the paint store and remember to stir frequently while using. Stain, like paint, is manufactured in batches and the batch number is recorded on the label. If you have purchased more than one can, you should box them (pour the contents of both, or several, cans into a larger container) to make sure that the color is uniform for the entire job.

Exterior stain is usually applied with a brush or it can be sprayed on if you have a large area to cover. It can be rolled on, but this is not as satisfactory as a china brush. If your stain is oil based, you should use a bristle brush, not nylon or polyester. We find that a synthetic bristle brush doesn't pick up and hold as much stain as a china bristle brush. We use a 4″ brush even on large areas such as a roof or shingle siding.

Before you start, you should know that staining is a messy job. It doesn't take much talent to wind up with spots on virtually every square inch of your body, especially if you're working outdoors, so dress down. And if you plan on holding hands with anyone that evening, wear plastic gloves while applying the stain. It's a good idea to wear plastic gloves anyway.

You should also remember to stir your bucket frequently because stain settles out more quickly than paint. If you don't keep the pigment suspended, you'll get color splotches.

The trick to using stain on exterior work is to apply it very liberally. Don't try to lay it off, just sock it on to whatever you're covering because covering is exactly what you're doing. The stain will penetrate on its own and provide the protection the wood needs. So just slop it down and spread it around a bit so that it doesn't run. Generally, the more you get on the surface, the better it is.

Since it is sloppy work, you should also cover anything that you don't want stained or spotted, windows, for example. That's why you should do the stain first. So that if you do mess up the trim, it won't matter all that much because you can paint over the stain spots.

Decking

In recent years adding a deck to the side or back of a house has become popular in our part of the country and probably in your area as well. We advise our paint store customers to stain rather than paint their decks. Paint will just "walk off" the deck floor and the stairs because of the foot traffic and the fact that these areas are exposed to the weather. For this kind of job we carry and recommend a decking stain. It comes in about ten different colors, even a bleached look if that's what you want. It works well, goes on easily, and looks good because it can tie in with or contrast the rest of the house.

Many decks are made with Wolmanized lumber which is treated with preservatives under high pressure to resist rot and decay. We recommend that you do not paint or stain Wolmanized lumber for three to six months. Let the wood weather a bit so the paint or stain will penetrate better, then treat as new lumber.

Creosote Stain

This is an old-fashioned wood preservative that is rarely used anymore. At one time it was used to preserve railway ties and fence posts or any wood that was buried in soil. It was very effective but miserable to work with because at best it not only gives off a horrible odor; on a hot day it emits fumes. I only mention it here because creosote is the exception to my statement that you can paint over stain spills on the trim.

Creosote stain spills will bleed through your paint, so if you do use it (and you probably shouldn't because it is illegal to use in some states), wipe it off immediately if you spill any on the trim. Use a cloth first, then thinner, and get as much off as possible. It also irritates the skin, so by all means use gloves.

Cement Stain

This is made for concrete decks, foundations, or stairs, and is used on new concrete that has been "cured" but not painted. Concrete should cure, or age, for at least three months before staining. Stain works much better than paint because stain penetrates whereas paint will wear off, especially where there is high foot traffic. However, concrete must be etched before either staining or painting. Etching is done with muriatic acid (which is dangerous to handle), followed by a thorough rinsing with water. Allow to dry out, then stain.

Fences

We have found that the best way to paint a fence, especially a picket fence, is to have one person on each side, working closely together. When you paint a slat in the fence, the paint has a tendency to "crawl" around to the other side and when it sets up or hardens, you have what we call a "fat edge." And you know what the neighbors would say if you had a fence with fat edges.

SUMMARY

Interior

- In a new room, stain and varnish woodwork before painting walls and ceilings.

- Stain is usually best applied with a bristle brush. Then wipe off the excess with a clean rag.

- Use sealer for soft wood such as pine.

- After staining, sand (and dust) before applying polyurethane or varnish.

■ Check chip chart carefully before buying stain. Purchase a small amount and experiment on scrap wood to get the exact shade desired.

Exterior

■ On siding, stain is best applied with a bristle brush, but it's a messy job so dress down.

■ Stir bucket well and often; stain settles quickly.

■ Use liberally — as the label says.

■ Use stain on a deck rather than paint for longer wear.

10
Refinishing Floors

EQUIPMENT NEEDED

☐ Floor sander

☐ Sandpaper (coarse, medium, & fine grades)

☐ Edger

☐ Screwdriver

☐ Hammer and nail set

☐ Hook scraper (with file to sharpen)

☐ Shellac or polyurethane varnish

☐ Stain (if necessary)

☐ Dust mask

☐ Safety goggles

Your floor is the last thing to be done in any room; it comes after painting walls, ceiling, and trim, or after papering, if that was your decoration decision. It's probably just as well. If floors came first, you might very well quit before you worked up to the walls, let alone the ceiling. Without trying to be cute . . . sanding a floor ain't easy. It's a job that is probably best left to a professional because it requires specialized equipment, it's dusty, and it

takes a bit of muscle to handle the power sander. That said, here's how to do it.

Let's assume that you've bought an old house and have been redecorating it. You and your spouse have been doing most of the work yourself, and so far everything is going along great. Hard work, but very rewarding.

You have saved the floors for last and had planned to install wall-to-wall carpeting. Except now you're out of money. And, even though the floors look a mess, underneath the mess is the original pine floor. If only you could restore it to the way it looked when the house was built. Well, of course you can . . . and the first thing you do is rent a sander. Actually two sanders.

A floor sander has a drum about eight inches wide. At the bottom is a plate with three screws which must be loosened to secure the sandpaper that fits around the drum. The screws must then be tightened flush with the machine so you don't gouge the floor. This is important to remember since you'll be changing paper often throughout the job.

When you rent the machine, make sure that you get three different grades of sandpaper: coarse, medium, and fine. It will probably come with the rental, but you should make sure you get enough. You can always return the unused paper.

The sander is the big machine that will handle the bulk of the work, but you will also need an *edger*. This is a smaller machine, a rotating disc, about eight inches in diameter, that works in close to the base of the molding and into the corners. But even this won't reach into the tight corners, and here you must use a hook scraper. This is the same tool that is used on the house exterior. It will work better if you keep it sharpened with a file. (It doesn't have to be so sharp that you can shave with it, but it will work better with an edge.)

You should also know this about the floor sanding machine: it's heavy. The weight varies by manufacturer and some brands are heavier than others. There are generally two types: the professional model (which weighs in excess of 100 pounds and does a better job), and the homeowner rental model which is considerably lighter. You can probably get somebody at the equipment rental shop to help you lug it to your car, but when you get home you might need help lifting it out of your luggage compartment and certainly carrying it upstairs, if you're going to do a second floor room. In addition to being noisy (forget about listening to your stereo while you work), it is dusty. You should wear a dust mask and safety goggles, the kind that fit over prescription glasses if you wear them.

Make sure everything is out of the room before you start because you won't want to stop and start the machine. If you're doing more than one room, start off in the room with the least noticeable floor, i.e., the bedroom before the living room. This is to give you confidence and sharpen your operational skills. Handling a floor sander does take a bit of practice. You should also look over the floor for protruding nails. If you discover any, use your hammer and nail set to drive them below the surface of the floor, otherwise they will surely tear your sandpaper. Some homeowners also remove the round molding that goes along the baseboard next to the floor. This will allow you to get the big machine in closer to the edge. (But make sure you don't leave any nails.)

Start off using the coarse sandpaper. It's worth noting again to make sure that the three screws at the bottom of the disc are flush. After you're plugged in, make sure that you work ahead of the cord and take great care that you don't run the machine over it. (I know that sounds obvious, but you will be concentrating on the floor and it's easy to forget about the cord.)

DON'T MAKE WAVES

You must sand *with* the grain of the wood; don't go across the floor. If you do, you'll make waves. Literally. It's also very important to keep the machine moving because if you stop, even for a split second, you'll dig a hollow in your floor. Again . . . sand with the grain . . . and keep moving . . . back and forth. Yes, I know it's tiresome, but don't stop now. The coarse grain sandpaper digs into the wood and loosens things up. When you notice that it isn't sanding as well as it did, it's probably time to change the paper. Move the machine to a place that you haven't sanded yet and turn off the machine to replace the paper. You might use three or four pieces of coarse sandpaper before you finish the room. (It should be noted that the professional *is* able to work against the grain when it suits his purpose, but the best rule for the homeowner is to avoid this.)

Then use the edger, with its coarse grain sandpaper, to work along the baseboard. Because it's smaller and lighter than the sander, this machine is much easier to handle, but it, too can dig a gouge in the floor. After the entire floor has been sanded, you might have to remove the existing finish in the tight corners with a scraper.

Next, repeat the operation using medium grade sandpaper. At this point, you have probably developed the knack of handling the floor sander, but don't get overconfident. It can turn on you in a flash and take a bite out of your floor. One of our customers told me a story that's worth passing along. After he was set up, with his rented sanding machine in the middle of the floor, he turned on the switch and overloaded the current which tripped the breaker.

The sander went off, but the switch was still on when he went down to the celler to throw the breaker. When the current came on, the sander took off like a jet across the floor, smashed a hole in the wall, and then kept growling away, digging a deep gouge into the floor. And all of this in just the time it took him to get back upstairs from his basement.

It will take several pieces of medium sandpaper and at least the same amount of fine paper. Thus the entire operation is repeated three times . . . including the use of the edger. You'll have to sand by hand the tight corners where you worked with the scraper, again following the same progression of sandpaper.

You might run across a bad spot or stain that simply won't sand off. (One example is dog urine.) The stain must be removed or it will show through your new finish. The easy solution is to try chlorine bleach (which you probably have at home). This isn't easy to control, but it might work. If not, you can buy some oxalic acid at your local paint store. Oxalic acid can be made into a paste which is much easier to control. You can actually outline the spot you want to remove and bring the floor back to a uniform condition. Check with the salesperson at the paint store for instructions on using oxalic acid.

After the entire room has been sanded . . . three separate times . . . all of the existing finish has been removed and you are down to the bare wood. Before you do anything, vacuum the floor thoroughly; the room should be dust free.

FINISH THE JOB

Now you apply your finish. You have several choices. One factor, of course, depends on the kind of wood that was used to make your floor. In older homes, floors were frequently made of pine; newer homes usually have oak flooring. Pine develops a rich patina that looks great but because it's soft, the floor shows its wear and tear and bruises. It's also difficult to refinish because your sander can cause waves unless you're very careful. Oak floors are much harder, and consequently easier to sand. (It's a good idea to find out what kind of wood you have before deciding whether to sand or not.)

If you want to keep your floor light — as you might, if it's oak — you can just apply a clear polyurethane varnish. You can also use a shellac but it does not wear as well as the polyurethane. For what it's worth, we prefer the polyurethane. Roll on one coat and let it dry overnight. Then sand lightly by hand using a fine grade of sandpaper. You can also rent a much lighter sanding machine, much like a polishing machine, for this job.

After removing the dust from the floor, apply the second coat of polyurethane. When the second coat has dried overnight, your floor is finished and you can move in the furniture.

If you decide you want a darker floor, you can stain it. Before you start, read Chapter 9 for full particulars on staining woodwork. The procedure is the same for your floor. Check out the colors at your paint store and use the chips to determine the shade you want. If your floor is pine, you might want to get a brand that contains a sealer or conditioner.

Your stain is best applied with a 4″ bristle brush, (if it's oil base stain), and as we've mentioned earlier, working with stain is a messy job. Take great care that you don't splash the walls or woodwork. It's also a good idea to test before you apply the stain. If the color is a bit too light, it's easy to apply a second coat, but if it's too dark, it's hard to make it lighter.

You will also note that once the stain has been applied and dried, the floor will feel rough because the grain has been raised. It must be sanded smooth before the next step. After the dust has been removed with a vacuum, you can apply a coat of polyurethane. Then sand lightly, remove the dust, and apply a second coat. Your floor will not only look beautiful, but with normal, routine care, it will last for years and years.

THE EASY WAY OUT

There is a shortcut version to the above. First, you clean the floor by removing all the wax that has been accumulating, probably for years. This can be done with a number of cleaners on the market. We use a "wax-off" product that removes the wax by dissolving it with water. Then lightly scrub the floor with steel wool. All the wax and dirt must be removed. After this is done the floor should be allowed to dry thoroughly because there are crevices in the floor boards where water will collect, even though the surface of the floor is dry. When the old wax has been removed, you'll probably notice bare spots in the floor. This is where the original finish has worn off. The best way to get an even finish is to apply a coat of white or orange shellac over the entire floor.

Since shellac dries very quickly, in a couple of hours (or less), you can apply a coat of wax and buff it. You now have a floor that looks beautiful in a newly decorated room. It won't stay that way as long as a floor that has been sanded and refinished, but the procedure can be repeated in a year or two.

If your in-laws are coming to visit and you can't spare the time to shellac the entire floor, you can retouch the worn spots with shellac and then wax the floor when the retouched spots are dry. You should also remember that a newly waxed floor is very slippery and warn your in-laws to be careful.

IT'S WORTH THE EFFORT

It really is. An exposed wood floor adds a unique warmth and charm to a room. It depends on your lifestyle, of course, and I know it's additional work to maintain, but if you have beautiful floors (or floors that can be made beautiful) that are now covered with wall-to-wall carpeting, think about it. More and more of the new homes now being built have unfinished floors that must be covered with carpeting. If you have a floor to show off, why not do it?

I know of one couple who built an expensive new home and had carpeting installed throughout the entire house. Three years later they removed the carpeting and put down a parquet floor. They find it makes the house much more spacious and is easier to take care of than carpeting.

SUMMARY

- Rent floor sanding machine and edger.
- You will need three grades of sandpaper — coarse, medium, fine.
- Start with coarse sandpaper, and sand with the grain of the wood.
- Use edger along the baseboard.
- Remove stains, if any, with chlorine bleach or oxalic acid.
- Vacuum up dust and apply finish. This can be polyurethane varnish or stain and polyurethane. Stain is messy — take care that you don't spatter walls.
- Shortcut version: Remove wax and retouch worn spots only. Then shellac and wax.

11
How to Figure a Job — Inside and Out

NOTE: Some of this material is also covered in other chapters.

Most paint contractors use a rule of thumb formula for figuring the amount of paint needed for a residence. (For interior commercial work, such as a factory, we figure square feet and many contractors use an estimating guide.) My father and I invented the formula that we use for estimating the amount of paint needed for the exterior of a house. It couldn't be simpler and it has always worked for us. We allow one gallon of paint for each room of the house and add an additional gallon for each hallway.

For example, if you have a two story, six room home, you will need eight gallons of paint for your prime coat. This includes an upstairs and a downstairs hall. You should only need seven gallons for your finish coat because the prime coat will take more paint than the finish coat. You should also compensate for the fact that:

■ Shingles take more paint than clapboard.

■ Bat and board, which is usually rough cut, will use more paint than clapboard.

■ Foundations and stucco will use more paint than clapboard.

MEASURING — EXTERIOR

The most accurate way to determine the amount of paint you will need is to figure the square feet on each side of your house. To do this, multiply the length times the height for each side.

With a tape measure, measure the length of the front of your house in feet at the ground level. Measure the height up to the roof line. The length × the height = square feet. Multiply that figure by two to get the back of the house and you now have the square foot measurement for two walls.

Then figure the sides of your house. Measure the width along the ground, in feet, and the height from the ground level, or top of the foundation, to the roof line. Multiply these two figures to get the square footage of one side. Double that for both sides. Add the square footage figures of all four sides for the total.

NOTE: You might have to measure each wall separately. If any of your four walls has an additional feature such as a porch, greenhouse, or add-on shed, take that into consideration for your final total.

Next, measure the gable, which is the triangular part of the wall under a pitched roof. Multiply the height by the base and divide by two (because it's a triangle). The base is the same as your ground line measurement.

If you can't get a tape measure from the roof line to the peak, you can figure the gable height this way. Measure one of the clapboards at ground level in inches, then multiply this by the number of boards and divide by twelve to get the height in feet. If your house has shingles, use the same technique.

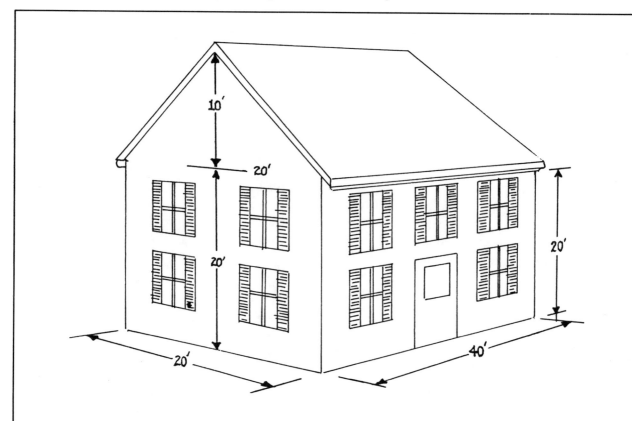

Formula for Measurements Shown Above

Front: 40′ × 20′ = 800 × 2 (front & back) = 1,600 sq. ft.
Side: 20′ × 20′ = 400 × 2 sides   = 800 sq. ft.
Gable: 10′ × 20′ = 200 × 2 sides = 400 sq. ft.
     ÷ by 2 (or triangle is ½ square)   = 200 sq. ft.
          total 2,600 sq. ft.

Assuming one gallon of exterior paint will cover 350 sq. ft., you would need 7½ gallons. (2600 ÷ 350 = 7½ gallons.)

Our rule of thumb method of figuring comes out to about the same figure if we assume that there are three rooms downstairs, three rooms upstairs, and two hallways, or a total of eight rooms. At one gallon of paint per room, we're right on the money with an additional half gallon of paint for safety.

It's actually much easier to do than to explain; the diagram will simplify the procedure further.

You now have the total square footage of your house. Don't deduct for doors and windows. The label on every one gallon can of paint will tell you the number of square feet that particular brand of paint will cover under ordinary conditions. Divide that number (say 350 square feet) into your square foot total of all sides and you have the number of gallons you will need for the entire house. (NOTE: This number will depend on the porosity of the surface.) Keep in mind that this is the number of gallons you will need for each coat; you will probably need a coat of primer and a coat of finish paint.

For painting trim, our rule of thumb is two gallons of paint per coat for the average six room house. This might include windows and sashes, two doors (front and back), fascia (edge of the roof to cover the rafters), and cornice return at the base of the gable. We generally paint the leaders (downspouts) as well to tie them into the house so they don't stick out like a sore thumb. If you have shutters, say six pair, you will need approximately an additional gallon. Here again, I'm talking about one gallon for prime and an additional gallon for finish paint.

It should be noted that latex paint doesn't go as far as oil base paint and the manufacturer's instructions on the latex paint label say "apply liberally."

If you have a detached garage, make certain to include the additional square footage of exterior wall space. Use the same procedure, of course, to measure the garage.

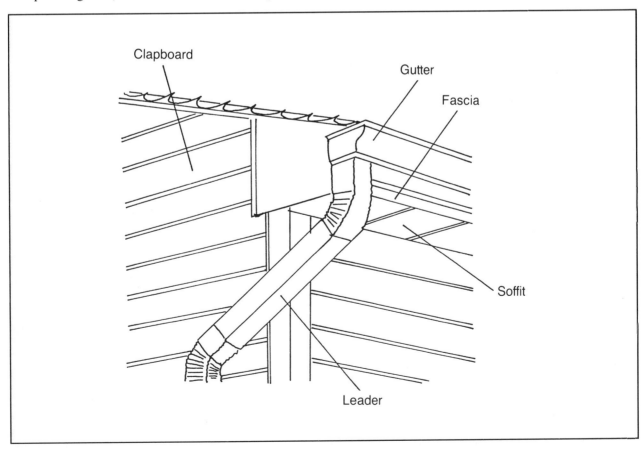

Clapboard

Gutter

Fascia

Soffit

Leader

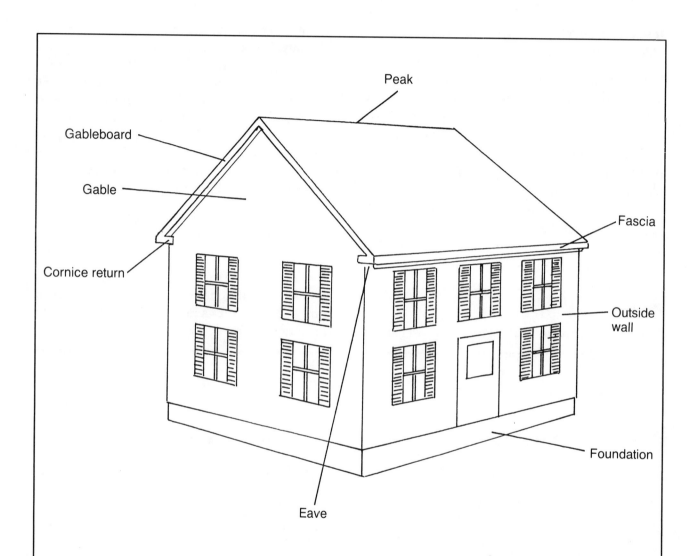

Basic Parts of a House

Peak — Top part of the roof. Also called the Ridge.
Gable — Triangle-shaped part of the wall under a pitched roof.
Eave — Lower part of the roof that hangs over the wall.
Fascia — The board or band that covers the ends of the rafters at the eaves.
Soffit — The part under the roof overhang.
Leader — Downspout.
Lintel — Beam or stone bar over the top of the window.

MEASURING — INTERIOR

Our rule of thumb is approximately one gallon per coat for painting the four walls of an average 12′ by 14′ room. We figure one gallon will cover one coat of two ceilings. Approximately one quart per coat will cover the trim of an average room.

To figure exactly: Measure the height of your room, in feet, from the top of the baseboard to the ceiling. Then measure the length of the longest wall and multiply that figure by the height for the number of square feet in the first wall. Multiply that figure by two for both walls. Then figure the width by the height for the shorter wall, multiply by two, and add all four walls for the total. Don't deduct anything for the windows and doors.

Check your total room square footage against the paint can label. Err on the side of having more paint than you'll need, and buy an additional quart rather than take the chance of running short.

Unless yours is an unusual or extra large room, there is no need to figure the trim. One quart per coat per room should cover two windows, two doors (closet and entrance), and baseboards.

Method of application is a factor in determining how much paint to buy. Spraying uses the most paint, using a roller the next, and brushing the least. Most people, homeowners and professionals, roll on interior walls and ceiling paint. (Closets and bathrooms might be exceptions.) We almost invariably brush the trim paint.

HOW LONG WILL IT TAKE?

Most homeowners want to know. However, it's a very difficult question to answer becasue it depends on the person doing the job, the size of the house, the condition it's in, the equipment being used, and certainly the weather, if it's an exterior job. And that doesn't even take into consideration the number of coffee breaks you might take, Hav-

ing said all that, not addressing the question would be a copout. So here goes.

We have devised a rule of thumb formula that states: one professional painter can do in one day what a hard-working homeowner team can do in two days. Obviously, the formula doesn't hold true if the homeowner is a little old lady with back problems and the painter is a twenty-two year old overachiever. But it will give you some idea as to how long it will take.

Interior

Assuming an average 12′ × 14′ room has been prepped, the furniture has been removed, and the floor covered with a dropcloth, a professional painter should be able to paint one coat on the four walls and ceiling plus the trim in one day. Add two additional hours for the closet if it's a bedroom. That's one day for the undercoat and a second day for the finish coat.

A homeowner team of husband and wife could do the same job in one day for the undercoat and a second day for the finish coat. Cleaning up and returning the furniture would certainly be overtime.

Both of these situations demand that everything is ready and that no one goofs off.

Exterior

Certainly no homeowner likes to think that his or her home is average, so I'll use the word "typical" to describe a six room, two story, approximately thirty foot high clapboard house with an attached garage. The house has already been washed so a professional painter should be able to scrape and prime one side in 1½ days. He should be able to caulk, putty, and finish coat that same side in another 1½ days. This would be a total of three days per side or twelve days for the entire house. A homeowner should figure on doing that side in three days for the prime coat and another three days for the finish coat, or a total of twenty-four days to cover the entire house with two coats of paint. Twice as long as the painter. (It could very well be 2½ or even three times as long because a professional painter has all the necessary equipment at hand, especially the proper extension ladders.)

Again, these are pretty rough calculations because there are many factors to consider with exterior work. And certainly a painter wouldn't prime one side and then put on the finish coat. He would logically prime all four sides before applying the finish coat.

A homeowner might well ask, "If it takes this long — about four weeks — why should I even bother to do it myself?" The obvious answer is cost. You could save yourself a bundle. How big a bundle depends on the labor costs in your area. I mentioned earlier that our typical house would require eight gallons for the primer and seven gallons for the finish coat. Fifteen gallons multiplied by $15.00 per gallon is $225.00. To round out the figure, I could include brushes, mineral spirits, putty, and caulking and make a total of $300.00 for paint and materials.

In our area the job described above, including paint, could run as high as $3,000.00. If you could do the job yourself in twenty-seven days, you'd save $100.00 for each day that you worked.

In your area the figure might be as low as $50.00, but my point is simply that you can save money by doing it yourself, which is the whole purpose of this book. And you certainly shouldn't project these figures and say: "If I can save myself $100.00 a day by painting my own home, maybe I should go out and start painting other people's houses at $100.00 a day." Apprentices don't make that kind of money.

SUMMARY

Exterior

■ Measure the house exterior with a tape measure to get the total number of square feet.

■ Divide total square footage by the average coverage listed on the paint can label to determine the number of gallons needed.

■ Rule of thumb: One gallon of paint for each room, plus an additional gallon for each hallway.

■ Shingles and rough cut bat and board use more paint than clapboard.

Interior

■ Rule of thumb formula: One gallon per coat for painting the four walls of a typical 12′ × 14′ room. One gallon will cover one coat on two ceilings. Approximately one quart per coat will cover the trim of a typical room.

■ For exact measurements: Multiply the height in feet of the wall (from baseboard to ceiling) by the length to get the square footage of one wall. Multiply this by four walls to get the total square footage for the room. Don't deduct anything for windows and doors. Check your total room square footage against the paint can label.

■ Err on the side of buying more rather than less.

How Long Will it Take?

■ Rule of thumb: One professional painter will do as much work in one day as a homeowner team does in two. Or, a painter should paint one room (one coat on four walls and ceiling, plus trim) in one day. A homeowner husband and wife team could do the same in one day.

■ Rough estimate: A professional painter might paint a typical house (wash, scrape, apply prime and finish coats), in twelve days. The same job might take a homeowner twenty-four days.

(See page 147 for a blank copy of this form.)

Paint Planner

Date: 3 - 4 - 89

Room FAMILY ROOM

	Total SQ FT To Cover	Coverage Per Gal.	Gallons Needed	Cost Per Gal.	Total Cost For Room
CEILING First Coat	140	300 - 400	1/2	13⁰⁰	13⁰⁰
Second Coat (if needed)	140	SAME	1/2		
WALLS First Coat	384	300 - 400	1	17⁰⁰	17⁰⁰
Second Coat (if needed)	384	SAME	1	17⁰⁰	17⁰⁰
TRIM First Coat	—		_1_ Qt. ☑ ___ Gal. ☐	8⁰⁰	8⁰⁰
Second Coat (if needed)	—		_1_ Qt. ☑ ___ Gal. ☐	10⁰⁰	10⁰⁰
Closet / Pantry First Coat			___ Qt. ☐ ___ Gal. ☐		
Second Coat (if needed)			___ Qt. ☐ ___ Gal. ☐		
Other					
Totals	524 + TRIM		1 CEILING 2 WALLS 2 QTS. FOR TRIM		65⁰⁰

(See page 149 for a blank copy of this form.)

Room / Cost Estimator

Date: _6/3/89_

Room _LIVING ROOM_

	Size of Room	Total SQ FT	Est. Gals. Needed	Cost Per Gal.	Sub Total
WALLS	length __14__ ft. width __12__ ft. height __8__ ft.	_416_ sq.ft.	__1__ Gal	$ _17⁰⁰_	$ _17⁰⁰_
	2nd coat (if needed)		__1__ Gal		$ _17⁰⁰_
CEILING	length __14__ ft. width __12__ ft.	_168_ sq.ft.	_½_ Gal	$ _13⁰⁰_	$_____
	2nd coat (if needed)		_½_ Gal		$ _13⁰⁰_
TRIM	Windows __2__ Doors __2__ Baseboards __4__		__1__ Qt. ☑ Gal. ☐	$ _8⁰⁰_	$ _8⁰⁰_
	2nd coat (if needed)		__1__ Qt. ☑ Gal. ☐		$ _8⁰⁰_
Closet / Pantry	Walls & Ceiling		__1__ Qt.	$ _9⁰⁰_	$ _9⁰⁰_
	Door & Baseboard	_FIGURED ABOVE_	_____ Qt.		$_____
Floor	length _____ ft. width _____ ft.	_____ sq.ft.	_____ Gal	$_____	$_____
Totals for Room		_584_ sq.ft.	_6_ Gal	$ _72⁰⁰_	

(See page 151 for a blank copy of this form.)

Room Painting History   MASTER BEDROOM (Room)

		Color Formula	Brand Name	Qty. Used	Cost	Who Painted	Date	Hours Spent
CEILING	Undercoat	WHITE	COLOR-GLO	½ Gal.	TOTAL 13.⁰⁰	RMS	5/17/89	
	Finish Coat	WHITE	COLOR-GLO	½ Gal.		RMS	5/18/89	
WALLS	Undercoat	337 SEASHELL	COLOR-GLO	1 Gal.	17.⁰⁰	RMS	5/18/89	
	Finish Coat	337 SEASHELL	COLOR-GLO	1 Gal.	17.⁰⁰	RMS	5/19/89	
TRIM	Undercoat	WHITE	COLOR-GLO ☐ Oil ☑ Latex	1 ☑ Qt. ☐ Gal.	8.⁰⁰	HWS	5/18/89	
	Finish Coat	WHITE	COLOR-GLO ☐ Oil ☑ Latex	1 ☑ Qt. ☐ Gal.	10.⁰⁰	HWS	5/19/89	
CABINETS (Wood work)	Undercoat		☐ Oil ☐ Latex	☐ Qt. ☐ Gal.				
	Finish Coat		☐ Oil ☐ Latex	☐ Qt. ☐ Gal.				
	Stain		☐ Varnish ☐ Polyurethane	☐ Qt. ☐ Gal.				
Closet / Pantry		337 SEASHELL	COLOR-GLO	1 ☑ Qt. ☐ Gal.	9.⁰⁰	RMS	5/18/89	
Other				Total	Total 74.⁰⁰		Completed 5/19/89	Total
Comments								

12
Care of Brushes, Paint, and Ladders

BRUSHES

We carry the same line of brushes in the store that we use on the job — top of the line. Because a brush is a relatively expensive tool, it's foolish not to take care of it. The best place to start is on the job, while you're using it. Here's the procedure we follow.

Never let a brush dry out. Don't lay your brush down on a piece of paper or on the lip of the can if you need to stop painting (or switch to a different brush), even for a short time. When a brush starts to dry out it becomes stiff and hard on the edges and by the heel, under the metal part. A brush used with latex paint seems to harden faster than oil, but once hard and dry, an oil brush is very difficult to clean.

We keep the brush wet on the job by putting it into a can of the same paint we're using. We sometimes use a separate can with about two or three inches of paint; just enough to keep the brush soft and wet until the next use. Lower the brush into the can and let it stand on end. You can do this when you knock off for lunch, but don't leave the can or your work bucket sitting in the sun if you're doing exterior work. Put them in the shade, or indoors if the weather is hot.

Some people dunk the brush in a can of water when not in use. Don't. The water will thin the latex paint which could run down your arm while you are painting, especially on overhead work. And don't soak an oil brush in water because the bristles are porous and will swell. Why not just use the paint you're working with?

Latex Brushes

At the end of the day, we quit about fifteen minutes early to clean brushes. Latex brushes are easy to clean. We wash them in laundry tubs with clear running water or keep changing clean water in buckets. Wash them at least three times. Work the paint out with your hands, particularly out of the heel. We also use a comb which is made to fit tight up against the heel. After the brushes are thoroughly clean, wrap each in a piece of newspaper or the container it came in, then lay it flat to dry overnight. You can also hang it by the hole in the handle.

Oil Brushes

If you are using alkyd, or oil base, paint, your job is more difficult because you must use mineral

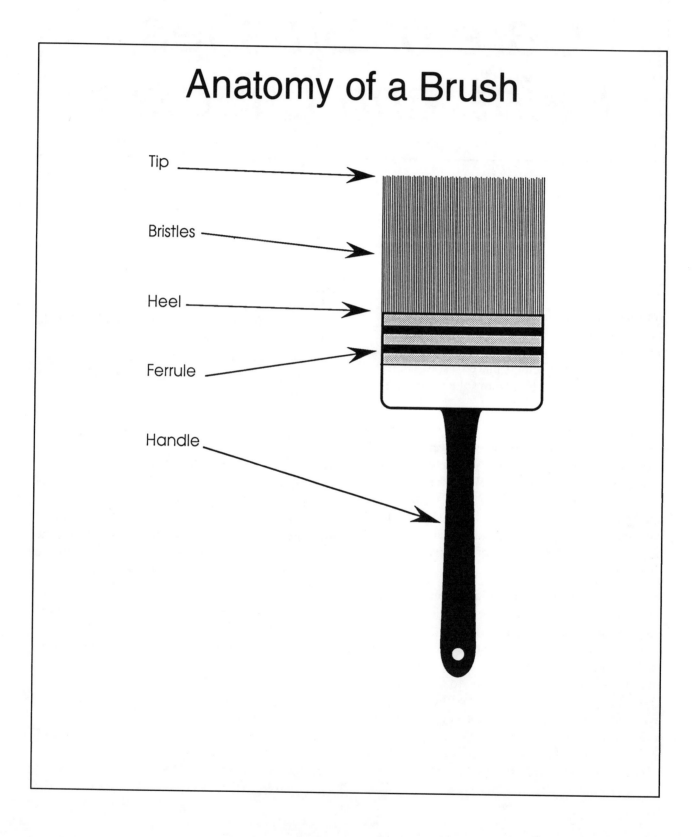

Anatomy of a Brush

Tip

Bristles

Heel

Ferrule

Handle

spirits or paint thinner to clean your brushes. However, the procedure is the same. Pour thinner into a bucket and move the brush up and down, then pour off the dirty thinner and replace it with clean thinner. Repeat three times to make sure the paint is out of the brush. Then wash it, very briefly, just dunking the brush in warm, soapy water to remove the thinner. Wrap in the original container or a piece of newspaper, and lay flat. The dirty thinner can be reused later when the paint settles to the bottom of the can.

If you're sure that you are going to use the brush the next day, you can speed up the process by rinsing once with thinner and wrapping the brush in its container or newspaper. Then insert the brush upright into a can of thinner to prevent it drying out overnight. The next day, before using, spin the thinner out of the brush to make sure it's dry.

Ten Do's and Don'ts for Brush Care

(Courtesy of Purdy Paintbrush Co., Portland, OR.)

1. Don't soak brushes in hot solvents or commercial liquid brush cleaners. Excessive soaking is the fastest way to ruin a brush. Clean brushes immediately after using instead of soaking them.

2. Don't soak brushes in water. Pure animal hair bristles (used for oil base paint) soaked in water will absorb and swell. Eventually the bristle will dry and shrink, causing the brush to fall out of the ferrule. Even synthetic brushes can be severely damaged by soaking in water.

3. Don't "hammer" the brush on any surface. Hammering can bend the ferrule, resulting in large chunks of brush falling out. Spinning the brush is the best way to remove paint residue.

4. Don't use the brush edgewise. Resist the temptation to use your larger brush on its edge; pick up a smaller, angular trim brush.

5. Don't allow your brush to "finger." Fingering is the separating of filaments. It is caused by only half-cleaning the brush and allowing it to dry with paint residue holding the filaments crooked. Use a brush comb specially designed for brush cleaning.

6. Don't stand a brush on its painting tip. Always place the brush in its original wrapper or wrap it in newspaper. Then hang it up or lay it on its side.

7. Clean each brush thoroughly and according to its need — soapy water for latex brushes; thinner for oil brushes.

8. Use each brush for its intended purpose. Match the brush to the paint — synthetic brushes for latex paint; natural bristle brushes for oil base paint. Match the brush to the project, using the right size for the area being painted.

9. Don't interchange a synthetic brush between oil base and latex paints without a thorough cleaning.

10. Realize the value of each brush. With paintbrushes, you get what you pay for. Team up a good paint and a good brush and you'll get a good job.

PAINT

This bears repeating: Don't work from a full, freshly opened gallon can of paint. It's impossible to stir it properly without first pouring off some of the paint into another container. Even though your paint can might have been recently shaken at the paint store, pour the contents of the can into a clean bucket, six quart size or larger, so that the paint can be completely stirred before using. If you don't have a larger bucket, use an empty gallon paint can, provided it's dry, and pour part of the

A Typical Can of Paint

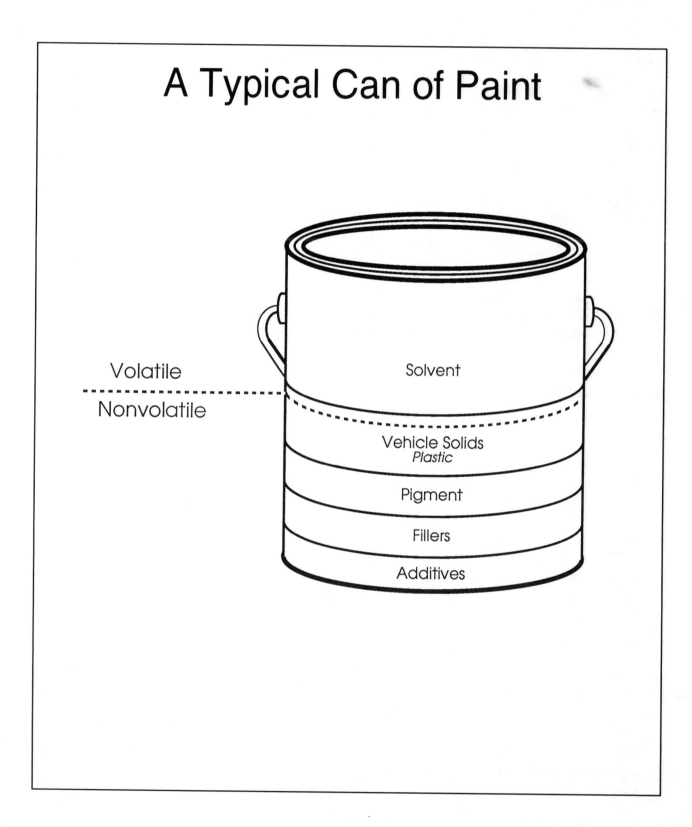

Volatile

Nonvolatile

Solvent

Vehicle Solids
Plastic

Pigment

Fillers

Additives

new paint into the empty can, then box it by pouring back and forth until the entire gallon is thoroughly mixed.

This advice holds for both latex and oil base paints, but proper stirring is especially important with an alkyd or oil paint.

We work from a work bucket which is usually less than half full. And we always make sure that the wire bales (the handles) are secure, especially if we're using a gallon can as a work bucket. This is particularly important if you're working from an

extension ladder because the can is suspended from a rung of the ladder by a pothook and the wire handle.

It's good procedure to keep the lip of the can clean as you are working, but before you store the can for any length of time, it's important to make sure it's clean so that the lid seals tightly. And you should store the paint in a warm place. Cold weather can freeze latex paint and will cause alkyd paint to congeal or thicken.

After a job is finished, we always leave spare paint

HOW TO READ A LABEL ANALYSIS

High Quality Interior Latex Flat
(Good scrub resistance, good wet and dry hide, good stain removal quality, good application properties, excellent adhesion)

Totals (Wgt. Basis)

			%	Lbs.
PIGMENT 42.7%				
Titanium Dioxide	47%	. . . .	20% Titanium	2.42
Silica & silicates	38%	. . . .	23% Filler Level	2.78
Calcium Carbonate	15%			
	100%			
VEHICLE 57.3%				
Non-Volatile Vinyl Resin	17%	. . . .	9.7% Binder Solids	1.17
Water	66%			
Glycols & Additives	17%			
	100%			

Weight per gallon: 12.1 lbs.

Low Quality Interior Latex Flat
(Poor scrub resistance, poor wet hide, good dry hide, poor stain removal, fair application properties, moderate adhesion properties)

			%	Lbs.
PIGMENT 42.99%				
Titanium Dioxide	15%	. . . .	6.45% Titanium	0.75
Calcium Carbonate	30%	. . . .	36.5% Filler Level	4.27
Silica & silicates	55%			
	100%			
VEHICLE 57.10%				
Vinyl Resin Solids	10.41%	. . . .	5.9% Binder Solids	0.69
Water	84.00%			
Glycols & Additives	5.59%			
	100.00%			

Weight per gallon: 11.7 lbs.

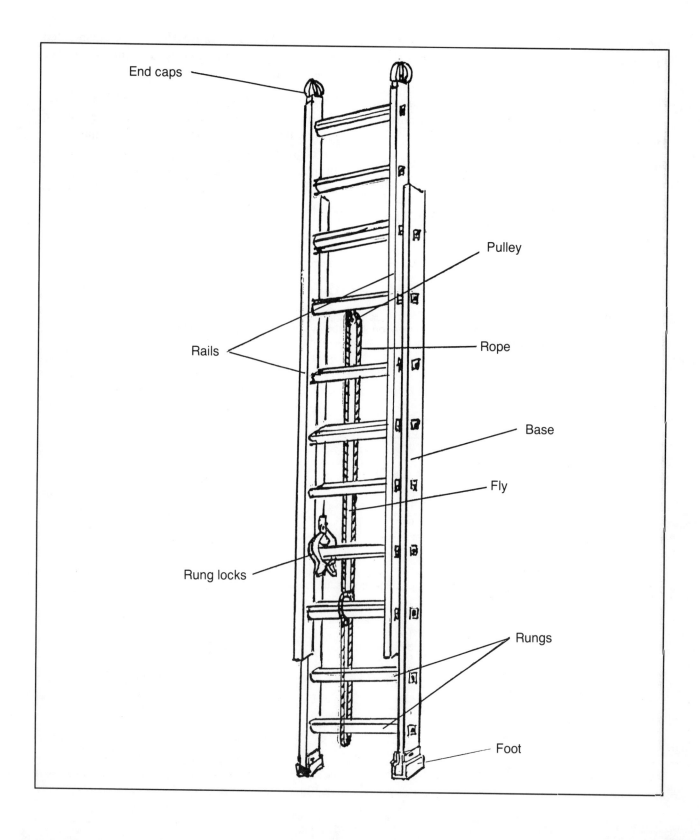

for our customers so that they can touch up if necessary. We write on the lid the room in which the paint was used. It's a good idea to include the date as well.

If you have to do touch up, before opening your can of stored paint, take it back to the paint store and ask them to shake it. Strain the paint before using because it will have a tendency to "skin" up. Latex is not as bad as oil paint, but even so, it could develop little particles which shouldn't end up on your walls. We use pantyhose for straining, but you can also buy a paint strainer. If the paint has been stored in a cool place, let it warm up before using. Lower temperatures will cause oil paint to thicken and become "ropey" rather than flow out to a nice, smooth finish.

Most homeowners probably have a stash of partially used gallon cans of paint in the garage or cellar. While an unopened can has a shelf life of many years, an opened partly full can of paint will deteriorate over a period of years. And if the lid hasn't made a tight seal, the storage life is considerably shortened. As a rule of thumb, if the paint is three or more years old, it should be properly disposed of, and you should purchase new paint for your next job.

LADDERS

A painter spends a good part of his work day on ladders, depending on the job, of course, and whether he's working indoors or out. We treat them with great respect and caution. It goes without saying that when you buy a ladder, you should read the manufacturer's instructions carefully. Then make sure the basics are secured to the ladder to reread each time you use it.

When the extension ladder is placed alongside the wall to be painted, we use two people to raise it. The first person braces the ladder's feet with his feet, while the second raises the top of the ladder and walks it forward. While he's pushing the ladder up and away from him, the first person is pulling it up toward him. When it's vertical, he pulls the rope until it reaches the required height, the rung locks are secured, and the rope tied off.

It is safer, and certainly easier, to raise an extension ladder with two people, but if you must do it alone, this is a good procedure. Make sure the fly — the part that goes up — is in the down position. Then brace the feet of the ladder up against the wall you're working on, and push it up until it's in an upright position. Make sure that there are no obstructions (like wires) above you. Then brace the ladder and raise the fly by pulling on the rope until you reach the required height. (Old gloves, rags, or towels secured to the end caps prevent scratching of the wood surface.)

Make sure the rung hooks are properly secured before tying off the rope. Then pull the ladder back away from the wall until you have a safe angle. The usual rule of thumb is to see that the ladder is pulled out from the wall approximately one-fourth of its height. Obviously, common sense and topography should be factors. And certainly your ladder should be rigid and sturdy enough to support you safely. Most important: make sure you have a firm, level footing and that there's no danger the legs could slide or sink in soft earth.

We use extension ladders ranging from twenty to thirty-six feet long. For heights below twenty feet, we use what is called a push-up ladder; an eight foot ladder that extends to twelve feet, and a six foot ladder that extends to nine or ten feet. However, a twenty-four foot extension ladder should allow you to reach most parts of a typical two-story house. Unusual features or an especially high peak might require a longer ladder. Whatever the height, you should never stand on the top three rungs when the fly is extended.

Even though your extension ladder is probably aluminum, it does require maintenance. One area to check frequently is the rope that raises and lowers the fly. If it's worn, it could break when you are raising the fly which would then come crashing down. If there's the slightest doubt, replace the rope with a new one. It's also a good idea to put a couple of drops of oil on the pulley so the rope rides freely and easily.

You should also check for cracks along the rails, especially where the rungs fit into the sides. Also make sure the feet are free of mud or dirt and that they swivel and level properly. If your rung locks have springs to snap over the rungs, give them a drop of oil to help prevent rust. If the ladder has curves or bends in one of the sections, this is probably caused by a drop. Cracks could develop as a result.

A good extension ladder is an expensive investment, so don't store it outdoors for any length of time. While we're working on a house we leave our ladders until the job is finished, but each night we lay them down, one on top of the other, and cover them with a tarp. Then they're returned to indoor storage. With proper care, an aluminum ladder should last for years and years. Unless your neighbor borrows it and doesn't give it the same care that you do. In that event, let him read this chapter.

Summary

Brushes

■ Never let a brush dry out. Keep a brush wet on the job in a can of the same paint you're using.

■ Thoroughly clean latex brushes with warm soapy water; oil brushes with thinner.

Paint

■ Stir paint thoroughly before using.

■ Strain paint before using if it has been stored for any length of time.

Ladders

■ Use caution and common sense when raising and positioning an extension ladder.

■ Check the ladder for cracks and worn rope regularly.

■ Don't store your ladder outdoors.

13
Equipment

EXTERIOR EQUIPMENT

Rather than list the equipment needed to paint your house, let me run through the equipment that we carry on our truck. Then you can use this section as a memory jogger next time you start a painting project or as a permanent list of equipment that you might want to acquire over the years.

Stepladders

We carry both four foot and six foot stepladders. For inside work we prefer metal; for outside work, wood. We feel safer with wood because wood ladder legs don't sink into soft ground as easily.

Extension Ladders

These are used primarily for exterior work, of course, and we use aluminum ladders exclusively because they're easier to handle, especially the longer lengths. Ladder lengths can be misleading. For instance, a twenty foot ladder will not get you twenty feet off the ground. There is a three foot overlap between the base (the lower half that remains on the ground) and the fly (the upper half that extends). You also lose an additional three feet because you should not climb on the top three rungs. Thus a twenty foot ladder will put your feet fourteen feet off the ground. However, your body height will add four or five feet, so that the average person could comfortably reach up to about eighteen or nineteen feet. Before buying an extension ladder, ask about the actual standing height so that you can be sure of reaching your highest point. You should also take into consideration that the ladder's reach will be reduced by about a foot when it is leaned into position against the siding. The traditional safe angle for the ladder is achieved by setting the base of the ladder at a distance from the wall that is equal to approximately one-fourth the height of the extended ladder.

We carry 14', 20', 24', 28', and 40' extension lengths. Since we have more than one person working on an exterior job, we need at least two of each. This also allows us to "put up a rig," as we call it. It's actually an aluminum plank that comes in 14', 16', 18', or 22' lengths. These are used with ladder jacks which fasten to the ladder rungs and siderails, and form a simple platform suspended from inside the two ladders. For commercial interiors with high ceilings we use a wood 6' extension plank that pulls out to ten feet; this is also suspended between the two ladders.

Dropcloths

We use canvas dropcloths because they're easier to work with and they're cheaper in the long run. We carry two types: the runners, for halls and stairways, which measure 4' × 16' or 18'; and the room size, which run 9' × 12', 12' × 14', or 16' × 16', depending on the need. We also use plastic sheets, but not if we have to walk on them. They're handy for covering a window or a drape that we don't want to take down. Plastic sheets are slippery when wet and they pool spilled paint. They can also be dangerous on a bare floor. However, they are considerably cheaper than canvas dropcloths, and you can also buy disposable paper dropcloths.

Brushes

Paint and brushes are a professional painter's livelihood. We would be doing it the hard way, but a painter could still do his job and earn a living without using anything else. Our need and use of brushes is somewhat different than the average homeowner's, so the following might not be of great value to you. But for what it's worth, here's how we make use of our brushes.

Each of our painters carries a set of three brushes on the job with him: a 2" (or 1½"), a 3", and a 4" brush. (Actually two sets; one is china bristle, the other polyester.) At the shop, we have light brushes and dark brushes. A light brush is used for painting white, gray, or any pastel color. It would be used from one day to the next by washing it out in the evening and again in the morning to get the color completely out of the brush. We have other sets of brushes for deeper colors such as darker grays, greens, reds. The same procedure is used for these.

When any of our light or dark brushes become worn, we use them for dark paints such as barn red, porch floors, or black shutters. And finally, when they become stubby, we use them for tar or asphalt. We can use them again and again and just let them sit in the asphalt or in thinner until they are needed.

A set of three brushes will allow you to paint anything. As we mentioned earlier, bristle brushes should be used for oil base paints. (You can use a polyester or nylon brush but you won't pick up as much paint, and you don't have as fine a tip.) You should use a polyester or nylon brush for latex paints. If you use a bristle brush in a water base paint, it will ruin the brush by causing it to puff out.

Scrapers

Our painters carry a hook scraper and a chisel knife, which is usually a stiff blade about an inch and a half wide. We also have a putty knife and a flexible blade spackle knife and use either, depending on the job. It's important to sharpen the scrapers from time to time. A simple file works fine.

Rope

We use rope to tie back the bushes so that we can get to the house exterior to paint at the ground level. We also tie the ladders in place if we're working on the roof. You should make it a point to check the rope on your extension ladder from time to time. If it's showing signs of wear, replace it. We use sash cord for most of our needs, although not for extension ladders. This takes a stronger rope. We like to use hemp because it's easier to handle. Many new ladders are using plastic rope which is strong but thin, which means that the pulleys are also narrow. When replacing rope on your ladder, check out the size of the pulleys as well as the condition of the rope.

We also carry wooden stakes to tie shrubbery back (if there are no trees handy) and hedge clippers to cut back any bushes that might be rubbing up against the house.

Stir Sticks

Remember to ask for one or more whenever you buy paint. There are very few substitutes if you don't have one. And if you're working with a five gallon can for boxing several gallons of color paint, you'll need a longer, sturdier stick than the gallon size stirrer. We use a "paddle" that is specially designed for stirring five gallon batches of paint. We also use a piece of interior trim about three feet long and three inches wide.

Power Washers

Some professional painters swear by them. We have often considered getting a power washer, but have decided against it each time. We don't carry them in the store because they are uneconomical for typical homeowner use.

The basic washer uses water mixed with a detergent. It does a good job of cleaning and removing loose paint.

An operator who doesn't know how to use a power washer risks injury to himself and/or the building. You must direct the water at an angle. If you hit the side of a building straight on, water can penetrate the cracks and wet down your insulation. When that happens, there is a good possibility that peeling will occur after that side is painted. You can also break windows and remove skin, or worse, if you hit yourself.

However, we do use them on some jobs, especially where there is a heavy collection of mildew at the second or third floor heights. And we do recommend power washing on unpainted brick houses and stucco siding. Over the years, an accumulation of dirt will collect on a stucco house especially, and it takes a power washing to flush out the dirt. We recently suggested that a customer rent one for his stucco house, after giving him some tips on how to use it. After the washing, he was so pleased with the results that he decided not to paint.

Power Roller

We've tried them but we don't carry power rollers in our shop and don't recommend that our customers run out and buy them. Not so much the cost — which runs somewhere around $100 — but because of the problems with using them.

You've probably seen power rollers or received ads with your gasoline credit card invoices. The roller is hooked to a small tank with a hose. This allows a constant supply of paint and eliminates the need to bend down to the tray. Clogging is often a problem and the flow of paint is not always even. Also the wash up of the tank and head roller can take more time than you save.

Miscellaneous

Extension ladder

Push-up intermediate ladder

Six foot stepladder

Four foot stepladder

Brushes — 4″, 3″, 2″ bristle brushes for acrylic, oil base paint; 4″, 3″, 2″ polyester or nylon brushes for latex, water base paint. (We prefer polyester.)

Sandpaper — We use a coarse grade for exterior and a fine or medium grade for interior trim.

Pothooks — Metal hooks, necessary for hanging your paint bucket on the ladder rung.

Work bucket — Plastic pail with a sturdy handle. This should have a reinforced top so it won't stretch out of shape when filled with paint. We also use a dry, empty gallon paint can with a sturdy handle. We never use the bucket that the paint comes in. The gallon can is too full to stir properly, so part of it must be poured off into a work bucket. We also paint from the smaller work bucket. We use a five gallon can to box the paint when using a color paint.

Scraper — Hook type, with single or double edges.

Helpful Painting Tools

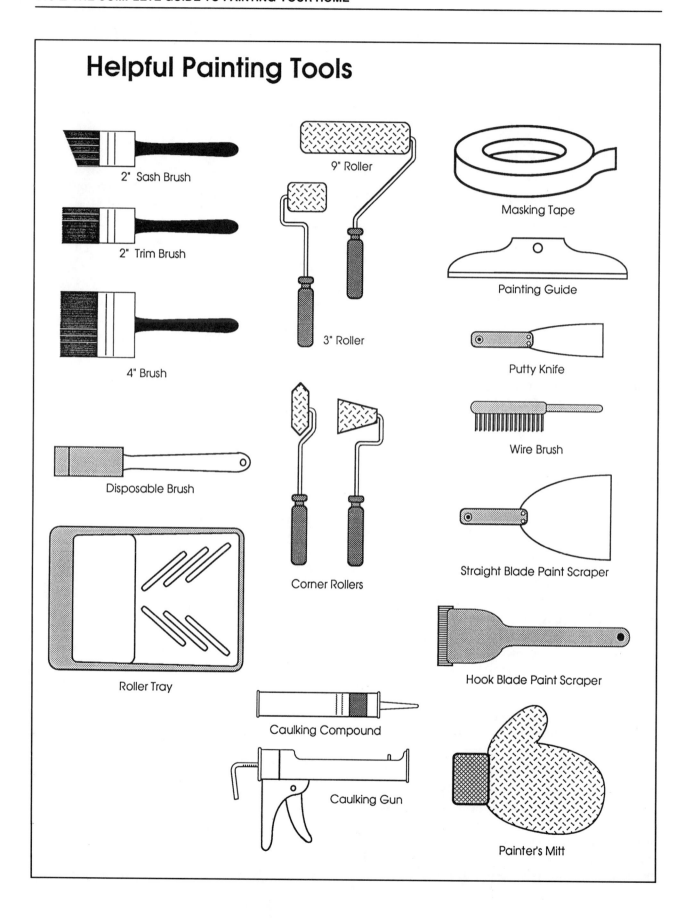

2" Sash Brush

2" Trim Brush

4" Brush

Disposable Brush

Roller Tray

9" Roller

3" Roller

Corner Rollers

Caulking Compound

Caulking Gun

Masking Tape

Painting Guide

Putty Knife

Wire Brush

Straight Blade Paint Scraper

Hook Blade Paint Scraper

Painter's Mitt

Chisel knife — Heavy duty.

Sandpaper — Coarse.

Duster — For sweeping dust after sanding or scraping. We use a flexible 4″ paintbrush.

Putty — Can or plastic container. For filling holes or fixing windows.

Caulking — For patching, tightening cracks.

Caulking gun — Use with caulking.

Dropcloths — Lightweight canvas is better; it's reuseable and won't burn bushes and shrubs. Plastic is lightweight and inexpensive, but can be slippery and might burn shrubs.

Ropes — Sash cords used with wood stakes for tying back bushes.

Garden trowel — For moving dirt away from foundation to allow painting.

Screwdriver, hammer, pliers — To pull nails or make simple repairs while painting.

Ladder blocks — These are 2″ × 4″ or 2″ × 6″ pieces of wood used to level out the ladder on a slope.

Sawhorses — They're handy when painting shutters because you can work from a flat surface.

Razor blade holder — Great for scraping excess paint from windows.

Garden hose, scrub brush, bucket — For washing down the exterior siding.

Strainer — We use screen wire for straining exterior paint and pantyhose for straining interior paint; exterior paint is too coarse to strain through pantyhose.

Rags — An essential to carry for cleaning hands, spilled paint, and brush handles, especially when working above shoulder height.

Propane torch — For burning dried putty and paint to remove broken glass.

Flexible putty knife — For repairing glass.

Push points — Arrowhead shaped with push edge for repairing glass. These are better than old-fashioned glazing points.

Power sander — The belt or vibrating type; rotary sanders leave marks on wood. We use one for removing old paint. Also an extension cord and safety glasses.

Ruler — For measuring windows if you need to replace glass.

Saw — For cutting branches that have grown onto the roof or gutters.

Clippers — For cutting back bushes that have grown up to the side of the house.

INTERIOR

In addition to stepladders, brushes, work buckets, and dropcloths we carry:

Rollers and extension poles

Roller trays

Masking tape

Church key can opener — For cutting out cracks in walls or ceilings.

Sandpaper

Steel wool

Razor blades (in holder) — For scraping dry paint off window glass.

Scissors — Handy for places a razor knife can't get to.

Straight edge — Usually a piece of aluminum about six feet long. We use this to split the wallpaper when we have to cut a strip off one side of the paper while hanging.

Level — It's easier to handle than a plumb bob to draw straight lines to hang wallpaper.

Seam Roller — This is an important tool to roll down the wallpaper seam where the edges of the paper meet.

Clean 7″ paint roller — Very handy for papering, especially for sizing the walls. Sometimes we paste the paper with this roller which is better than a 9″ for getting between casings.

Plastic garbage or yard bags — For disposal of the old wallpaper being removed.

Screwdriver, hammer, pliers, scraper

(See page 153 for a blank copy of this form.)

Use This Tools and Equipment Checklist Before Starting Your Next Paint Job

Brushes

Bristle (for alkyd oil base paint)				Polyester / Nylon (for latex paint)			
Size	Qty.	Condition	Need To Get	Size	Qty.	Condition	Need To Get
1 1/2" or 2" Trim brush	1	GOOD	1	1 1/2" or 2" Trim brush	1	OKAY	2
3" Doors Wide Trim				3" Doors Wide Trim	1	NEW	1
4" Siding			2	4" Siding			

Tools & Equip	On Hand	Need To Get	Tools & Equip	On Hand	Need To Get
Interior			**General Tools**		
Drop cloth	1	1	Mineral Spirits/Turps	1 QT.	1 GAL.
Masking Tape		2 ROLLS	Pot Hooks		✔
Nail Set	✔		Putty	SOME	✔
Roller(s)	1	1	Rubber Gloves	✔	
Spackle		1 CAN	Sand Paper	✔	
Spackle Knife	✔		Scraper	✔	
Steel Wool	✔		Scrub Brush	✔	
Tray	✔		Stirrers		✔
Exterior			**Wall Covering**		
Buckets		1 5 GAL.	Carpenter's Level	✔	
Caulking		✔	Plumb Bob		
Caulking Gun	✔		Scissors	✔	
Chisel Knife			Seam Roller		✔
Garden Hose	✔		Size		✔
Safety Glasses		✔	Smoother Brush		✔
Extension Ladder		BORROW	Sponge	✔	
Step Ladder	✔		Razor Knife & Blades	✔	
			Water Bucket	✔	
			Wallpaper Table	✔	
			Water Box		✔

(See page 155 for a blank copy of this form.)

Home Owners Inventory - Paint Supplies

Exterior Primer
Latex ☐
Alkyd ☑

Brand _COLOR-GLO_
Used for _HOUSE EXTERIOR_
Color / Tint _LIGHT GRAY_
New (Unopened) ☑
Used When ? _____
How much left ? Gal. _1_ Qt. _____
Condition _FINE_
Comments _____

Exterior Finish
Latex ☑
Alkyd ☐

Brand _COLOR-GLO_
Used for _HOUSE EXTERIOR_
Color / Tint _DOVE GRAY 717_
New (Unopened) ☑
Used When ? _____
How much left ? Gal. _1_ Qt. _____
Condition _FINE_
Comments _____

Exterior Trim - Primer
Latex ☐
Alkyd ☐

Brand _____
Used for _____
Color / Tint _____
New (Unopened) ☐
Used When ? _____
How much left ? Gal. _____ Qt. _____
Condition _____
Comments _____

Exterior Trim - Finish
Latex ☑
Alkyd ☐

Brand _COLOR-GLO_
Used for _DOORS, SHUTTERS, ETC._
Color / Tint _BLACK_
New (Unopened) ☑
Used When ? _____
How much left ? Gal. _____ Qt. _1_
Condition _____
Comments _____

Interior Undercoat
Wall ☑ Latex ☑
Ceiling ☐ Alkyd ☐

Brand _COLOR-GLO_
Used - room(s) _MASTER BEDROOM_
Color / Tint _337 SEASHELL_
New (Unopened) ☐
Used When ? _5/89_
How much left ? Gal. _1/2_ Qt. _____
Condition _OKAY_
Comments _____

Interior Finish
Wall ☑ Latex ☑
Ceiling ☐ Alkyd ☐

Brand _COLOR-GLO_
Used room(s) _FAMILY ROOM_
Color / Tint _452 WARM BEIGE_
New (Unopened) ☑
Used When ? _____
How much left ? Gal. _____ Qt. _1_
Condition _____
Comments _____

Interior Trim Undercoat
Latex ☐
Alkyd ☐

Brand _____
Used - room(s) _____
Color / Tint _____
New (Unopened) ☐
Used When ? _____
How much left ? Gal. _____ Qt. _____
Condition _____
Comments _____

Interior Trim Finish
Latex ☑
Alkyd ☐

Brand _COLOR-GLO_
Used room(s) _FAMILY ROOM_
Color / Tint _WHITE_
New (Unopened) ☑
Used When ? _____
How much left ? Gal. _____ Qt. _1_
Condition _____
Comments _____

14
Helpful Hints

The hints that follow are miscellaneous painting and decorating information that I learned the hard way.

SPILLED PAINT

Let's say that you have just spilled a can of paint on your nice new hardwood floor. The paint is pooling out a foot and a half in diameter. Your first impulse is to grab a rag and start mopping. But don't do that. Instead, use your brush and work from the outside in to contain the paint. Pick up the paint with your brush and wipe it on the inside edge of the can. Keep lifting up all of the paint that you can, then use a rag soaked with thinner (if oil paint; soaked with water if the paint is latex) and start cleaning off the paint from the floor. Keep at it, especially in the cracks, until all of the spill has been removed.

Immediate action will keep the spill from spreading. If you don't have a brush handy, use a broad knife or spackle knife to scoop up the paint until someone gets a brush for you. The paint that you picked up is still good, but it should be strained before using because you picked up dirt and dust from the floor.

If you're outside and the spill occurs on the lawn, you can get some of the excess up with a brush but most will be wasted. So will the grass under the spill. Cut out the sod at that spot and replace it with a square from some other part of the lawn. Don't reuse this paint.

A spill on an asphalt driveway poses a different problem. Here again, try to contain the paint with your brush, but don't mix this with the unspilled paint. You'll have to throw the asphalt tainted paint out because of the oils in the asphalt. Remove all of the paint that you can with thinner (if oil) or water (if latex) and then, when the paint has dried, get some asphalt paint or flat black paint and paint over the area. The shine will leave the spilled area after weathering for a few weeks and it will be barely noticeable. If this is not the case, you may have to apply driveway sealer to the entire driveway.

A roof spill is the worst. Pick up the paint with your brush and scrub the shingles with thinner or water until most of the stain is removed. Then mix or buy a paint the color of the roof — whether wood or asphalt shingles — and paint that spot to blend it in with the rest of the roof.

HOW LONG WILL PAINT LAST?

The shelf life for paint is years and years if the top has not been opened. We have used paint that has been stored for ten years and it was perfectly good. The real danger is that the can has rusted. When someone comes in with a severely rusted can for us to shake, we examine it very closely before putting it on the shaker because it could break and wouldn't that be a mess?!

After the can has been opened, it won't last more than two years, if that, and for latex probably less if it has been frozen. Most homeowners have paint left over from whatever job they worked on last. That paint is carefully saved for touchup. We always leave a supply of each color of paint to be used for this purpose.

Chances are it will never be used, and over the years, the old cans of paint accumulate. What to do with them? Dispose of them. Latex paint will freeze and the pigment will settle to the bottom. Oil paint won't freeze, but the pigment will settle to the bottom and a skin will form on the top.

WEATHER AND PAINT

Don't store paint in your garage if you live in the snow belt. Latex paint will freeze, of course, and oil paint will thicken. If you were to use it cold, you'd find it very difficult to work with. We warm up paint in the sun or alongside a heater if it even feels cold.

Most paint manufacturers print a warning on the label advising the user not to paint unless the outside temperature is at least fifty-five degrees (or whatever the specifics for that particular paint). It's a good idea to heed the warning.

DRESS THE PART

We have always worn overalls on the job and so do all of our employees — not because painters have always worn white overalls, but simply because they're designed to carry the things that painters use. When you go up on a ladder, you don't want to climb back down to look for a scraper.

If you plan to do much painting, overalls are worth the investment. You can also purchase disposable coveralls and throw them away when the job is completed.

We go even one step further; we wear clean overalls. Over a period of years, I have discovered how to get paint-spotted overalls clean. Put them in a bucket of water with bleach and let them soak overnight. Next day, rinse them out with clean water and put them in the washing machine with a good detergent. They'll come out soft and clean. The paint will still be there but bleached lighter, more like a stain, and the white will be clean.

KEEP THE LID ON

Don't work from your gallon can of paint after it's been opened and stirred. Pour about a quart into a work bucket, and put the lid back on the gallon can while you're working. You don't have to hammer it closed, but you do want to keep the air from hitting the surface and "skinning up" or forming a skin. If this happens, you should take time to strain interior paint through pantyhose and get rid of the skin. (Use a wire screen for exterior paint.) The closed lid will also keep out the dust and dirt. Remember to keep the paint where it's warm.

CLEANING ROLLERS

Leave the sleeve on the roller and place it on end in the roller pan. Take a putty knife and scrape the paint down the side of the roller into the pan. Turn the roller slightly each time to scrape all sides from top to bottom. (You'll be amazed at how much paint can be removed.) Now it will be much easier to wash the remaining paint out of the sleeve because much of it will have been scraped off.

After the roller has been washed with soap and warm water, rinse with clear water and spin dry. Store on end so any remaining water will drain off.

Cleaning a roller that has been used with oil base paint is a real mess for most homeowners. Unless you plan to use the same roller for the same paint in the next day or so, it's usually easier to dispose of it and start off with a new one next time you paint. If you do intend to use it the next day, scrape off the paint as explained above, but instead of washing it off with thinner, just place the roller in a plastic bag and store in a cool place. (I have put mine in the refrigerator, but never longer than overnight.)

Use the same technique to scrape as much paint as possible off your brushes before washing in thinner or water.

DON'T KICK THE BUCKET — REUSE IT

You can use a work bucket for more than one color. Let's say that a few days ago you were painting blue trim and today you have to use a white paint. If the blue paint in your work bucket is dry, you can feel perfectly safe in pouring the white paint in that blue bucket. The white paint won't soften the blue paint, and neither will any other color. You can also reuse your stirring stick, going from one color to another, if the stick is dry.

And while we're on the subject, empty gallon-size paint pails make excellent work buckets. It doesn't matter if you're using a different color paint, as mentioned above. You might also want to cut the rim off, as we do, with a stiff knife or can opener. By removing the rim, you now have a bigger opening for dipping the brush. These are much handier and less costly than plastic buckets. We've done this for years, inside and out. However, let me stress that the can must be empty and dry.

REMOVING PAINT FROM SCREENS

When you're painting above screens, it's a good idea to remove them or slide them up behind the glass if they're combination windows. If you're working above porch screens and you can't remove them (or don't want to), be very careful about getting paint on the mesh screening. It's difficult to remove.

However, if you do spatter paint, the procedure for removal from screening (either fiberglass or wire mesh) is this. Get to it immediately, while it's still wet. Once the paint has dried, it is much more difficult to remove.

Dip a dry paintbrush in a small amount of thinner or mineral spirits if it is oil paint, soapy water if latex, and rub the spot on both sides. The paint will come off, IF you get it while it's still wet. You do need a brush, however, to penetrate the mesh. It it's a bad spot, we use one man inside and another outside and have both try to rub the spot at the same time.

If the paint has already dried, you can remove much of it by using a pin and cleaning out the spots where the paint has globbed. And as a last resort, paint over the spot with black paint (if the screen is black) or whatever color matches.

When we have to paint the entire wire mesh screen, we use "painter pads" which measure about 2″ x 3″. We pour paint on the lid of a five gallon can (or use an empty pie pan), and pick up the paint with the pad and rub it over the wire screening, first one side, then the other. If the pad happens to touch the wood frame, we touch up with matching paint.

TOUCHUP

Many times we just do a touchup. In the fall we might check over a house and do a window sill here and there that needs painting. We color the paint so that it blends in with the slightly weathered paint on the rest of the house. This kind of checkup can get the house through another year or two before the entire house needs repainting.

Sometimes, just one side of a house needs to be painted. The house might be protected on three sides by trees with only one side exposed to the sun. Painting the exposed side can postpone repainting the entire house for several years.

When we paint just one side of a house, we usually wash any of the other sides that might have mildew. The only reason for mentioning this is because here the procedure is the reverse from the usual way of working. When washing but not painting, we wash from the bottom; the very bottom up. The reason for doing this is that if you washed from the top down, the water would streak the dry siding below and the streaks won't come out unless they are painted over. Which you don't intend to do. This is the only time you work from the bottom up.

BRUSHES

For latex paint use a manmade brush, i.e., polyester, nylon, or a combination of the two. A natural bristle brush used in latex paint will swell up, become limp, and "finger out" to the point where you'll have to throw it away or use it as a duster.

For oil base paint, use a natural bristle brush for best results. The absolute best is a china bristle brush. A manmade brush can be used with oil paint, but it won't carry as much paint or lay on as smoothly as a natural bristle brush.

GUTTERS

When you're priming and prepping the house and up there on the ladder anyway, it's a good time to clean out the gutters and downspouts. If the downspouts are clogged, you might have to take them down and tap them until the clogs fall out, or flush them out with a garden hose.

BACKPRIMING

The next time you replace an outside wood step, paint the underside as well. This is what we call backpriming. It keeps the topside paint from peeling because it helps to hold the moisture back on the underside.

GARAGE DOORS

Overhead wooden garage doors frequently peel even though the siding is still in good condition. The principal reason is that moisture collects on the inside — the unpainted side. On a hot summer day, the sun beating on the exposed garage door draws the moisture through the door toward the outside surface. This moisture pushes the paint off the surface and the paint peels. The simple solution is to paint the inside of the door (one coat) when you paint the outside. It's also a good idea to raise the door from time to time during the sunny parts of the day, winter and summer.

BUYING PAINT

We've said this before but it bears repeating: don't try to save money on paint, particularly exterior paint. Let's say you're repainting your house. By the time you've finished washing (to remove the chalk, dirt, and mildew) and scraping and sanding (to remove the loose or peeling paint), you've already put in a lot of time and effort. Painting your primer coat on the siding and trim, plus the finish coat on the siding and trim, will add considerably to those hours. In short, you have a lot of time invested. Now, if a top grade national brand paint could give you an additional year of protection over an on-sale "house brand" that you've never heard of before, wouldn't the slight additional difference in price make it worth buying the name brand? After you've finished painting your house, you won't want to do it again for a long, long time. A good quality, name brand paint will extend that time between paintings.

A professional painter figures the cost of the paint to be about 10% of the total cost. He'd really be shortchanging you if he cut his price by $25 or $50 and used a cheaper quality paint so he could pass those savings along to you. In paint, like most things, you get what you pay for. When you buy a good quality paint, you're buying a bargain.

DO YOU NEED TO PAINT?

Each side of your house (or garage) weathers differently; usually one side faster than the others. A professional painter will often tell a homeowner that only one side needs painting, the others just need to be touched up. This approach can protect your house for a few additional years until the paint has become chalky and all four sides need to be painted.

The side that weathers fastest usually receives the most sun, which has a far greater effect on a surface than cold, wind, rain, or the direction the house faces. The paint on those surfaces protected by trees will usually last longer and fade less than the sides having direct exposure to the sun. After carefully inspecting all four sides, if you can attend to the weather side and postpone painting the entire house, by all means do so, but follow these two important steps.

First, have the paint store color your new paint so that it matches the existing paint. The painted surface that's up there now has faded enough so it looks different than the tint formula you originally applied. Try to get a close match to avoid having the freshly painted side show up the rest of the house. And secondly, do the touchup work on the rest of the house. Just as one side weathers faster, the flat surfaces wear and fade faster than the wall siding, regardless of compass direction or sun. These are the areas where water collects such as window and door sills, porch floors, steps, etc. Obviously, here it's essential that you get a good color match.

Surprisingly, "overpainting" can sometimes do more harm than good. By this I mean applying a fresh coat of paint when the existing coat is still good. This is more likely to happen in the East where a very old house exterior has been painted a dozen times or more. The successive coats have built up until the original coat — which might have been laid down fifty or 100 years ago — has lost its adhesion due to the contraction and expansion of the wood. Then the sheer weight of the paint can pull off all of the layers.

WHY BOTHER TO PAINT?

There are plenty of impressive figures to prove that painting preserves wood and I suppose we've used a good many of them explaining to our customers, but there's nothing as convincing as our "demo" boards. A few years ago, we took two pieces of siding. We painted both sides of one and left the other unpainted. Then we threw them out behind the shop where they stayed on the ground in all kinds of weather for almost a year. The difference is amazing and never fails to convince skeptics. The unpainted board was cracked and discolored; the painted board was as good as the day we put it out to weather.

USING — OR NOT USING — MASKING TAPE

Professionals usually don't use tape, except for possibly one area which we'll discuss later. A painter's skill with a brush (and the fact that he has the right brush) allows him to cut in the walls without smearing the trim, and to paint the trim without messing up the walls. For homeowners, masking tape can be a blessing or a curse. However, if done right, it will save time and will give you a sharp-edged line between wall and trim.

Let's say you are masking the trim before rolling paint on the walls. First, there is a proper masking tape to use. There is a painter's masking tape which comes in different widths and is designed to pull up again. Then there's masking tape designed to stick tight. This kind of tape will often pull up the paint from the trim. If possible, use a painter's masking tape.

Second, and of great importance, the tape must be applied exactly right. By that I mean snug up against the wall. Any exposed area of trim will be covered with paint if you don't tape properly. (Knowing it's covered will give you a false sense of security when you cut in.)

And finally, painter's masking tape has glue on one edge only. Ordinary masking tape is difficult to handle without having pieces of it stick to itself or your fingers. The longer the strip, the more difficult it is to properly apply. There are tape applicators on the market that make this job easier and more accurate.

Professional painters usually only use tape while painting a room with stained trim. All trim is carefully taped with special attention given to the top of the baseboard. Spatter from your roller will surely accumulate on the top of the baseboard unless you cover it.

One trick that painters use when masking tape is not available is to apply a coating of oil to the top of the baseboard. We use linseed oil because it works best and we have it on hand. But you might use cooking oil or even petroleum jelly. You can use oil on the entire trim if you are careful not to get it on the walls because the paint won't stick to the oil. However, remember to remove it before painting.

PRIMERS AND UNDERCOATERS

To help you understand paint can labels:

A primer is generally used as the first or prime coat on exterior work. The finish coat is used on top of the primer.

Undercoater is the first coat used on interior trim or woodwork. It is specifically formulated for use over a hard and somewhat glossy surface. It dries flat, but provides a good bond for a glossy or semi-gloss finish coat. Just any old flat paint won't work as well.

Primer should also be used for the first coat of paint on new plaster or hardboard interior walls and ceilings. For repainting previously painted walls and ceilings, unless they are glossy, two coats of ordinary wall paint can be used, one over the other. The manufacturer's expression for a second coat that can be applied over the first (after it's dry) is "self-covering."

Don't paint gloss over gloss is a basic rule in painting. This is especially true with interior woodwork and exterior trim, but it also applies to exterior siding. You should first apply a primer (to siding) or an undercoater (to interior woodwork) because the existing worn but still somewhat glossy coat won't allow a good bond for the finish coat. You could sand the surface to rough it up and provide a better bond, but using a primer or undercoat is much easier and more effective.

What will happen if you do apply gloss on gloss is not catastrophic. Your walls won't come tumbling down, but the paint will chip, probably within the year, whenever you knock against it. Oil base paint is probably worse in this regard than latex.

Despite the above information, if you still intend to apply a glossy latex paint over an existing, somewhat glossy surface — and there's no way on earth that you are going to apply an undercoater — here's a "cheat" that will help. First wash the surface with Soilex or Spic and Span and allow to dry before painting. The clean surface, with all the surface dirt and grease removed, will provide a better bond for your latex finish coat.

But, once again, you should wash the surface first, apply the undercoat, and then the finish. By doing it right your paint job will look better and last years longer.

CARE AND CLEANING OF BRUSHES

Using the proper brush for the job speeds up your work; using a good brush makes your paint job look better. And since good brushes cost money, it's worth your while to know how to get the most wear from them.

Brushes Used with Oil Paint

When you have finished painting for the day, pour a small amount of thinner or mineral spirits into a small clean container such as a coffee can (for a small brush), a plastic bucket, or an empty, dry paint can. Push the brush up and down in the liquid to work out the paint. Pour this dirty liquid into a larger container. (You can save and reuse this after the paint has settled.)

Repeat the procedure with the same amount of clean thinner or mineral spirits. Then do it again, for a total of three rinses, and the brush should be clean. Use the original wrapper if you have it, or a piece of newspaper to wrap the brush. Then put the wrapped brush in a container (gallon paint can size) of clean thinner or mineral spirits. You can store at least a half dozen brushes in the same container. Many painters fashion a simple rig from a wire coat hanger to suspend their oil paint brushes so the tips don't touch bottom. Most brushes have a hole in the handle for point of purchase display; you can easily drill a hole if your brush doesn't.

Next day, or next time you use the brush, remove the excess thinner by shaking dry or spinning the handle between your hands. This is best done over an empty carton or garbage can because the spray will fly. (Painters often use a mechanical spinner.)

This storage procedure should be followed for overnight or short term use. For long term storage, wash the brush four times with clean thinner, shake dry, and immerse it briefly in warm soap and water. Shake dry, wrap in the original wrapper or newspaper, and lay flat. The brush may stiffen up slightly when stored for a length of time, however, it will soften up when used with paint. Before using, remember to spin the brush dry after soaking in thinner or water because a wet brush will dilute the paint and will also start to drip down your wrist when painting.

If you know for sure that you're going to use your brush the next day, you can follow this shortcut method. First, wipe out as much of the paint from your brush as you can. Then, insert it into a plastic bag large enough to take the entire brush including the handle. Seal it closed with a covered wire twist so that you can safely lay it flat. (When I'm working at home, I store the brush overnight in the refrigerator, but it doesn't earn me points with my wife.) Next day the brush will be soft and pliable. Just dip it in the paint and start working. However, don't use this technique if you intend to store the brush for any length of time; more than a few days will dry it out.

If you have let a good brush become hard, it's still possible to save it by using a liquid brush cleaner from your paint store. If there are several brands to choose from, you might ask the salesperson to recommend one. You must read the label carefully because the solution is usually so powerful that it could easily swell the bristles and puff out the brush. You should stay with it, working out the paint as it softens. Before buying, consider whether the brush is worth saving, and if the cost of the cleaning compound is not close to the cost of a new brush.

I know it's not always possible for a homeowner, but the best procedure is to make it a habit to clean up immediately after painting. Professional painters consider cleanup part of the working day and quit early enough to allow this before heading home.

Brushes Used with Latex Paint

This procedure is much easier and faster, because with latex paint you simply use warm soap and water. If a tub is available, you can hold your brush under the running water and knead it until all traces of paint are gone. Then spin dry or shake off the excess water, wrap in paper or the original wrapper, and lay flat.

OTHER CLEANUP

When using either oil base or latex paint, your work buckets should also be rinsed out after finishing for the day. First pour the excess paint into your larger container. Use thinner or mineral spirits for oil base paint or water for latex, and wipe the bucket clean. If you are using a five gallon container, use a clean brush to wipe down the sides with a small amount of thinner or water to keep the paint from hardening on the sides. Then replace the lid tightly.

Before leaving, we fold the dropcloths, stack the ladders, and remove tied-back ropes. It's a good plan to leave the work site in a clean and safe condition. It also goes without saying that you should use whatever solvent the paint is mixed with (i.e., thinner or water) to remove the paint from your face and body. Every paint store sells a very effective hand cleaner for this purpose; it's handy to keep around for grease and dirt as well.

REPLACING WINDOW GLASS

Just about every home has, or will have, a broken or cracked pane of glass somewhere. You can replace it with new glass without too much time and effort if you have the right tools, otherwise it will be a frustrating experience. You will need:

Propane torch

1½″ flexible putty knife

Putty

Glazing points

Replacement glass, cut to exact fit

If the glass is shattered in a wood window frame, work gloves might be helpful when taking out the shards after the putty has been removed.

NOTE: To simplify instructions, I am using the word "frame" to mean any part of the wood holding the window glass, both vertical and horizontal.

This is the procedure that we use. First, remove all curtains from the window, anything that could burn. Fit a small nozzle on the torch and light. Using a low flame, play the heat on the dried and hardened putty that must be removed before you can take out the broken glass. Heat a small section at a time, then, using your putty knife at a flat angle, get the corner of the knife under the putty and scrape it away from the frame. The heat softens the putty which makes it rather easy to remove. Don't try to muscle it out, let the heat do the job. When you come to a glazing point, switch to a stiff knife (if you have one) to pry it loose, or use a small pliers and extract the metal triangle.

Leave any broken glass in the frame until the putty is removed. The glass will keep your flame from working around to the inside and scorching the inside paint. (You can expect the exterior of the sash to be scorched.)

After the dried putty has been removed, use your knife to pry the glass loose from the frame. When this has been done and the frame is cleaned of dried putty (and glass), sand the frame smooth and repaint the scorched, raw wood before you put in the glass. If you don't paint first, the dry wood will absorb the oil from the putty. When this happens, the putty will crack and even fall out after a couple of years. It's better to wait a bit until the paint has dried, but professionals put the glass in place while the paint is still damp.

Now fit in the replacement glass and hold it in place with glazing points pushed in each side, and the top and bottom of the frame. Next, apply the fresh putty firmly with the tip of your knife, pushing it between the glass and groove. You will be working across the frame and, since your knife is only an inch and a half wide, you will need a number of knife loads, but you can easily control the amount of putty that you apply. Keep the back of your putty knife clean, otherwise the putty will pull out rather than spread.

Then, holding your knife at a forty-five degree angle to the frame, press tightly and make a long stroke along the frame, causing your dollops of putty to flatten into a long bead. Remove the excess and apply to the rest of the frame and repeat until the entire frame has been puttied. After the putty has dried, touch up the frame with the paint color to match the rest of the window.

15
Do It Yourself — with Others

If you are part of a group or organization with a repainting or restoration project, and you must (or simply want to) collectively do it yourself, I suggest that you talk it over with the owner of your neighborhood paint store before you start. This situation occurs at our paint store every year or so, but the most recent and the one that we're most proud of involved the restoration of an old church in Mt. Freedom, NJ, a small town about twenty miles from Madison.

A five acre parcel of land for "a church, manse, and burying ground," was purchased in 1820, and the church itself was built in 1823. ("A History of the Mt. Freedom Presbyterian Church in Randolph Township," by Dee Kojak.) It has been a place of worship for 165 years.

A new minister named Warren H. Crater proposed the restoration idea to his congregation of about seventy-five members. This was approved by the twenty-five or so active members and an eleven person work group committee was appointed. Pat Huck, a charming and energetic lady, was voted chairman and became my liaison.

When word got out about the restoration plans, a fund drive was started involving all residents of Randolph Township, church members, and families of those who were buried in the cemetery. Money was donated and the local Boy Scout troop gave the group a quantity of paint left over from one of their ventures. Fortunately, the color was a respectable pastel blue because, as one of the volunteers mentioned, "It settled any possible disagreement as to what the decoration of the church interior should be. All of us knew that the walls and the ceiling had to be blue." That was the status when Rev. Crater came in to the store and sold me on the premise that they had a big job and needed help. I agreed to go out with him to look it over and found that he didn't oversell the condition of the church. It really needed help. The blue paint on the walls had faded and the brown painted pews had been repainted many times, but were now so chipped that the bare wood was showing.

I explained to the work group that the pews should be tackled first. It would be a messy job since the many coats of paint would have to be removed and then stripped down to the bare wood. At this point, they had the option to stain or paint and they decided to paint. I told them to do it right, they would have to strip all the paint off, and then, after neutralizing the wood, they should apply two coats of undercoater and one coat of enamel finish. These were the original pews and I knew they

The congregational work group started restoration with the pews which were originally installed more than 150 years ago.

The congregation of the First Presbyterian Church in Mt. Freedom, New Jersey, have every reason to feel proud of their painting and restoration work, inside and out.

would look beautiful if they were done right. That's when the group (bless them), told me that the reason they decided to do it themselves was because they did want to do it right. They knew it was so labor intensive that they could never come up with enough money to have it done for them.

Part of the group came back to the store and bought some paint remover and a few knives and scrapers. Then I explained that the remover had to be laid on in one direction only. Their work schedule was to be one day a week on Saturdays. After a couple of Saturdays, I went back to see how they were coming and found that they were painting on the remover instead of laying it on in one direction. I got them straightened out on that and checked back, usually by phone, finding that they were making good steady progress. The same group showed up for work every week, and the thing that kept me interested was their determination "to do it right so it would last another 165 years."

When they had removed all of the paint from the wooden pews and applied two coats of undercoater, they felt the finish coat needed a professional touch. Unfortunately, our company was backlogged with months of work but I did find a good painter for them who was able to overcome any flaws they might have left. And it did look beautiful.

Pat Huck became a wonderful foreman because she devised a foolproof system for working with a group of dedicated amateurs painting pews, walls, and ceiling. She had everyone work on one job at a time. Everybody used remover and scrapers, everybody used undercoater until that job was done, then everyone used the same paint until the next job was completed. She bought only one kind of paint at a time so there was no chance that someone would pick up the wrong can. Unfortunately, the church interior walls were high enough so that scaffolds were needed to paint the ceiling. They hired a carpenter to repair the church steeple and some other work on the outside, and hired a couple of college students to paint the exterior. Eighteen months later the job was completed. Done right and without using church funds — though I suspect that the work group not only volunteered their time and talents but also dug into their purses for many of the expenses.

When the church was officially rededicated, my name was mentioned along with the names of the work group. I felt like I did at my high school graduation ceremony. If you're ever in the neighborhood of a Sunday morning, stop in and look it over.

16
The Way We Used to Do It

Of course it's not like it was in the old days when I broke into the painting business. It's a lot better . . . and easier. Material and equipment have greatly improved, probably because of the do-it-yourself market. For the most part, a paint job lasts longer and the color holds better.

Back then, people hired a painter because it wasn't as easy to get paint as it is now. "Package goods" paint was available, including basic colors, but you had to go to a paint store, and chances were the owner mixed your colors by hand. Rollers hadn't been invented yet, neither had latex paint. However, there is one area where there has not been any improvement. The old-time painter was better than his counterpart today. I say that flat out and I'll explain why.

"Back then," for me, was the late 1930s and early 1940s before World War II. As I mentioned earlier, my father was a painting contractor, that is, he had his own "shop," as a painting business was called. I could have gotten a steady job with him, but he wanted me to learn the way he had learned the business — through an apprentice program, which was then the usual way of learning a trade, any trade.

Becoming an apprentice was essentially making an agreement with an employer to work for him for at least three years, the usual period of apprentice training. In return, the apprentice would be taught the painting trade. In our area, this was usually handled through the employer's union which set the hours, pay scale, and duties. Hours were 8:00 a.m. to 4:30 p.m. with an hour for lunch (which most men packed in a black lunch pail), five days a week. However, the apprentice was expected to be the first man on the job in the morning and the last man to pack it in at night.

A typical shop consisted of four to six men, including the apprentice and employer. The apprentice worked with a different man each day, rotating through the week. This was a sound practice because each man had his own special way of doing a job. Being exposed to a variety of ways to do that same task allowed the apprentice to pick up or adapt the technique that worked best for him. Thus, each man was responsible for teaching the apprentice.

The pay was typically one-third of what a mechanic made. A mechanic was (and still is) a skilled professional able to handle any phase of painting. Our pay scale was basically the same within an area, although if an employer was swamped with work, he might raise his wages a bit so he could steal someone else's painters. Some men might spend twenty years working for the same boss, some would move on after a years or so to the next town where the grass was greener, and some were coast to coast drifters. The point is, a qualified painter could get a job virtually anywhere in the country during the spring, summer, or fall. During the winter in the East, work was often scarce and the top men got first call. An employer always tried to find work for his good men because if he laid them off, he might not be able to hire them back again when things picked up.

An apprentice's duties were anything and everything in the painting field, including how to make paint and mix colors. A great many painters used to buy white lead and mix their own exterior paint. White lead has been illegal to use since 1973, but then it was not only the basic but virtually the only exterior paint. We would buy a hundredweight keg (about 12″ high and 18″ across, with a crimped top) of white lead paste, put a scoop of this in a clean five gallon bucket, then thin it out with linseed oil and turpentine, plus driers, to get the consistency we wanted for the job required. A primer paint, for instance, was thinner than a finish paint. If it was color, we squeezed out an amount of color concentrate from a tube and mixed it in until the proper shade was achieved. We usually made up our paint the night before for the next day's work.

We also learned how to put up rigging and scaffolding safely, and how to handle extension ladders. The thirty and forty foot ladders weighed a ton and a half. I certainly don't yearn for a return to that kind of equipment.

There were no rollers either, so when interior paint was applied to walls and ceilings, it was with a 4″ or 6″ brush. And we used an oil base paint which smelled for days after. A flat paint was "swept" on, as we called it, with a semicircular motion. You couldn't leave the tiniest skip or it would ruin the whole ceiling — which meant that if a "holiday"

was seen the next day, you had to redo the entire coat of paint. A few experiences like this and you learned to be exact.

You learned how to do it right because most every job was done right — without shortcuts. New wood received three coats: two coats of primer or undercoater and one coat of enamel varnish. Everything was sanded between coats, all crevices spackled and all nail holes set. Old work, which is what we called painting over existing paint, received two coats, inside and out.

I mentioned earlier about painters looking clean on the job. It was customary at virtually every shop to arrive at work in the morning wearing your street clothes, and change into your work clothes before going on the job. If a newly hired man changed into dirty, paint-spattered overalls and shoes, the boss figured he was a slob. His reasoning was, "If you can't keep paint off your clothes, your work is probably sloppy as well," and no paint shop wanted that kind of reputation. After work, we returned to the shop to get cleaned up and change into our street clothes.

When a man became a painter, that's what he did and that's all he did. He didn't hire out as a carpenter on weekends. A man took pride in his work and spent an entire lifetime within that trade, buying a house and raising a family with a steady and secure source of income.

All of this lasted until a few years after the war. Then there was an explosion in the building trades. There was such a great demand for labor that unqualified "brush hands" began entering the painting field. Painting contractors were often offered a bonus by a homeowner who didn't want to wait his turn. Many simply tired of waiting, and hired people who claimed to be painters. The licensed trades such as electricians and plumbers were somewhat protected because there were building codes and qualified inspectors who were required to okay all such work, but even these fields were flooded with inexperienced people. Often inspectors didn't check the work because the job was never reported.

The unlicensed trades such as painters, masons, and carpenters were affected most by the work boom; perhaps painters most of all. Obviously they benefited, too. The old shops had more work than they could handle for a number of years. During that time, many painting contractors hated to answer the phone at night because they'd have to say no to a customer or ask them to wait an unreasonable length of time. So the unskilled "painters" moved in and took on jobs that they were unqualified to handle. They made mistakes that their customers paid for because they simply didn't know any better. Many of them required their customers to buy the finish paint to make sure the color was right. They hadn't learned because they hadn't had a professional teach them, and they hired helpers who knew even less.

And now we get to the purpose of this book. To learn a trade or mechanical skill, you should have a professional teach you by showing you how, with hands-on demonstration. Failing that, the next best method is to have a professional tell you how, with step-by-step instructions, as well as photographs and illustrations showing you how, as I've tried to do here. Not just the right way to do it, with reasons why, but also to tell you the tricks of the trade — things that I learned during a lifetime of "doing it right" — without shortcuts.

I still say if you can afford to hire a professional painter to paint your house exterior or interior, you should do it. And if you do, make sure that he is a professional by checking his references and talking with some recent customers. If you can't afford it, or if the job is small (lots of painters don't like to take on one-room jobs), do it yourself. Follow my instructions step by step, take it slow and easy, and you'll wind up with a professional job that looks good and will last for a long time.

As I stated earlier, the primary purpose of painting is to protect the surface underneath the paint. The second reason is to beautify. To the casual eye, a new paint job is so visible that the cosmetic effect overshadows the protection advantage. It invites compliments. People rarely say, "Hey, look at that great carpentry work," or "How about those pipes and conduits?" And conversely, if your house is not painted, sometimes the bank will call and say, "Let's get it painted soon and protect our mutual investment."

Text of an 1886, labor/materials invoice from Madison painting contractor John Gentzell to his customer, W. R. Ayers. Please note that a painter received something less than three dollars a day (the contractor had to make a profit). He also made his own paint, using white lead and basic colors.

MILLBURN June 17th 1886

Mr. John Gentzell to W. R. Ayers

May	4	1 days Painting	3.00
		25 lbs Lead	2.00
		1 gal Oil	.60
		½ gal Turp	.30
	5	¼ day Painting	.75
	6	¾ day Painting	2.25
		4 lbs Lind	.32
	7	2¾ day Painting	8.25
		100 lbs All Lind	8.00
		7 gal Oil	3.85
		3 lbs B Umber	.48
	10	1½ day Painting	4.50
		10 lbs Lind	.80
	14	10 lbs (?)	1.50
		½ gal Oil	.28
	28	½ day Painting	1.50
		100 lbs. All Lind	8.00
		5 gals Oil	2.75
		2 lbs B Umber	.32
		3 lbs Putty	.15
June	9	2 days Painting	6.00
		4 lbs B Umber	.64
		4 lbs Indian Red	.72
		1 lbs Putty	.05
		1 qt Oil	.15
		8 lbs Blue	1.60
	10	1 days Painting	3.00
	11	2¼ days Painting	8.25
	12	1¼ days Painting	3.75
		Graining Color	.25
	15	Varnishing Stain	.35
	14	½ days Painting	1.50

Received Payment $ 75.86

W. R. Ayers

Millburn June 17th 1886

Mr John Gentzell to
W.R. Ayers Dr

4	1	Day Painting	3.00
	25 lbs Lead		2.00
	1 Gal Oil		.60
	1/2 Gal Turps		.30
5	1/4	Day Painting	.75
6	3/4	" "	2.25
	4 lbs Lead		.32
7	2 3/4	Day Painting	8.25
	100 lbs All Lead		8.00
	7 Gal Oil	55	3.85
	3 lbs B Umber	16	.48
10	1 1/2	Day Painting	4.50
	10 lbs Lead		.80
14	10 lbs Prim Metalic	15	1.50
	1/2 Gal Oil		.28
28	1/2	Day Painting	1.50
	100 lbs All Lead		8.00
	5 Gal Oil	55	2.75
	2 lbs B Umber		.32
	3 lbs Putty		.15
9	2	Day Painting	6.00
	4 lbs B Umber		.64
	4 lbs Indian Red	18	.72
	1 lb Putty		.5
	1 qrt Oil		.15
	8 lbs Blue	20	1.60
10	1	Day Painting	3.00
11	2 1/4	" "	8.25
12	1 1/4	" "	3.75
	Graining Color		.25
15	Varnishing Door		.35
14	1 1/2	Day Painting	1.50
			$75.86

Recd Payment
W.R. Ayers

Text of Madison painting contractor P. H. Hanlon's bid on a residential job back in 1915. The bottom figure seems to say the cost would be $239 for three coats . . . which would be very unusual.

Mr. Herman Kluxen

    Dear Sir,

        We do hereby agree to paint the exterior of your house on Fairview Ave. with two coats of paint for the sum of one hundred and seventy nine (179) dollars.

        Yours truly,

            P. J. Hanlon's Sons

239. 3 coats (?)

RICHARD A. HANLON   ESTABLISHED 1870   HENRY J. HANLON

P. H. HANLON'S SONS
CONTRACTING DECORATORS AND PAINTERS

BRASS AND WOODEN CURTAIN POLES   WINDOW SHADES MADE TO ORDER

18 MYRTLE AVENUE
TELEPHONE 169-w

MADISON, NEW JERSEY, *Aug 3 1915*

Mr. Herman Klusen

Dear Sir,

We do hereby agree to paint the exterior of your house on Fairview Av., with two coats of paint for the sum of one hundred and seventy-nine (179) dollars.

Yours truly

P. H. Hanlon's Sons

2. 8 9. 3 coats

17
Most Common Mistakes

THE DOZEN MOST COMMON MISTAKES HOMEOWNERS MAKE, PLUS ONE

1. Trying to get by with one coat of oil base paint over existing oil/enamel coat on trim.

   Result: Your new coat of paint will start to chip when struck by a chair, vacuum cleaner, etc.

   Proper procedure: Apply undercoat (a flat finish paint) first to ensure good adhesion for your finish coat of enamel. **NOTE:** Two coats of oil base gloss enamel, one over the other, can cause the same problem.

   Rule: Don't paint gloss over gloss.

2. Opening a fresh can of paint and working directly from that can.

   Result: Drips and streams of paint on your hands, floor, and brush handle.

   Proper procedure: Pour paint into a larger bucket so you can stir properly or pour part of the paint into another bucket so you can dip properly.

3. Not washing surface before painting.

   Result: Poor adhesion.

   Proper procedure: Wash surface first with detergent to remove grease and dirt. This goes for both interior and exterior surfaces.

4. Using a cheap or improperly cleaned brush.

   Result: Ropey or rough finish. Sloppy work.

   Proper procedure: Try to use not only a good brush, but the right brush for the job. And make sure the brush is clean. (See pages 99–101 for the care and cleaning of brushes.)

5. Painting over a chalky exterior surface.

   Result: Your paint could peel from the chalky surface.

   Proper procedure: Prepare the surface first by washing and scraping where needed.

6. Failure to cover walks, bushes, floors, etc.

   Result: A sloppy paint job.

   Proper procedure: Use dropcloths inside and

out. Paint spatters are unsightly; spills are even worse. (And they do happen — even to professionals.)

7. Failure to ask knowledgeable people how to do the job.

Result: Quite possibly an amateur paint job that looks like you did it yourself.

Proper procedure: Unless you know what you're doing, ask your paint dealer for advice before undertaking a painting project. Also read this book and refer to it whenever needed. You'll save time and money . . . and wind up with a first class job.

8. Failure to place ladder properly.

Result: Spilled bucket of paint, or worse, an injured painter.

Proper procedure: You probably already know what you should do. Just don't get careless and take chances or shortcuts. Observe such precautions as these: Place ladder out from the wall, a distance equal to one quarter the height of the ladder. Make sure the legs are even and on a solid surface. Don't lean out too far and don't climb higher than the third rung from the top on an extension ladder, and don't stand on the top step on a stepladder.

9. Running out of paint or stopping in the middle of a wall instead of at the corner.

Result: A visible mark where the stop/start occurred.

Proper procedure: Make sure you have enough paint to complete the job. If you must stop, finish the complete wall.

10. Painting when the temperature falls below that listed in the warning on the can.

Result: Latex paint can freeze and peel off; oil paint may be dulled in spots or lose shine entirely.

Proper procedure: Follow instructions on the label.

11. Failure to stir paint thoroughly even though a new can has been stirred mechanically at the paint store.

Result: The top part of the can will be too thin (if latex) and too oily if oil base; the bottom of the can will be too thick.

Proper procedure: Stir thoroughly with paint stir stick and pour off part of the paint into a work bucket.

12. Failure to strain paint when it becomes lumpy or dirty.

Result: Dirt or lumps of paint will be applied to the surface and will look as if you have done a careless job.

Proper procedure: Strain interior paint through pantyhose and exterior paint through fine wire screen. (Oil paint often forms a skin after storage and this must be removed before use.)

13. This is the worst mistake. DON'T EVER DO THIS! Never attempt to move a ladder — step or extension — when the paint bucket is on the top step or hooked on the rung of the ladder. It not only can, but very probably will, spill. And won't that be a mess. It happens all the time.

TEN "DON'T DO ITS"

1. Don't paint over wax, grease, oil, dust, or dirt.

2. Don't paint over loose paint or a heavy chalk surface.

3. Don't use an oil base paint on a wet surface.

4. Don't work out of a full bucket (especially out of a newly opened can).

5. Don't leave plastic dropcloths on bushes or shrubs in the sun.

6. Don't place your ladder on or near an electric wire.

7. Don't mix oil and latex paints together.

8. Don't lay your ladder on a freshly painted surface.

9. Don't work directly over anyone.

10. Don't paint outdoors when the temperature is lower than the manufacturer's specifications on the label.

Glossary

Quick definitions of some common painting terms.

ALKYD — Oil base paint.

BASEBOARD — Wood board that goes around the room just above the floor and below the wall.

BLEEDING (through) — Discoloration or stain that comes through the paint such as those caused by smoke, water, tannic acid, etc.

BOX — To mix together, as paint from two or more gallon cans mixed in a five gallon can.

CAULKING — Filling openings with caulking compound.

CHALKING — Powdering surface; comes off to the touch.

CORNICE — Overhang of a pitched roof at the eave line, usually consisting of a fascia board, a soffit for a closed cornice, and the moldings.

CORNICE RETURN — Portion of the cornice that returns on the gable end of a house.

COVER UP — Placing dropcloths on walks, shrubs, floors, furniture, etc.

CUTTING IN — When using a roller, to paint a strip with a brush. Painting a small area along the wall/ceiling line to allow complete coverage of areas where the roller can't reach. Can also refer to bottom of wall along the top of the baseboard or cutting in a window or sash.

DECK PAINT — Enamel with a high degree of resistance to wear, designed for use on surfaces such as porch floors.

DRAGGING — Hard to brush paint.

DRYWALL — Interior covering material, such as gypsum board, which is applied in large sheets or panels.

EAVE — Margin or lower part of a roof projecting over the wall.

FASCIA — Flat board used sometimes by itself but usually in combination with moldings, often located at the outer face of the cornice.

FLASHING — Dead spots in shiny finish.

FLAT PAINT — Interior paint containing a high proportion of pigment and drying to a flat or lusterless finish.

FOUNDATION — Supporting portion of a structure below the first-floor construction.

GABLE — Portion of the roof above the eave line of a double-sloped roof.

GABLE END — An end wall having a gable.

GLOSS PAINT — Paint containing a relatively low proportion of pigment and drying to a sheen.

LAP — Where two coats of paint meet and overlap.

LATEX — Water base paint.

LINSEED OIL — A natural basic ingredient in oil base paints; now generally replaced by alkyd, a manmade oil.

LINTEL — Horizontal structural member supporting the load over a door or window.

MASKING TAPE — A sticky-backed paper used to cover areas which butt up against surfaces being painted, such as a window casing when rolling a wall or glass when painting a window frame.

MILDEW — Black stains (spores) on surface of paint.

MILK OUT — Squeeze out paint from brush or roller sleeve.

MINERAL SPIRITS — A thinner like turpentine used to dilute oil base paints or to clean brushes used with oil base paints.

MOLDING — Wood strip having a curved or projecting surface used for decorative purposes.

MULLION — Vertical bar or divider in the frame between windows, doors, or other openings.

PARTING STRIP — Small wood piece used in the side and head jambs of double-hung windows to separate the upper and lower sash.

PIGMENT — Powdered solid used to color paint or enamel.

PLASTER — A fast-drying powder used to fill large openings or cracks.

PRIMER — First coat to prepare surface for finish coat; usually used in reference to exterior coverage.

PUTTY — Type of cement used in sealing glass to sash, or filling small holes and crevices in wood.

RAIL — Cross members of panel doors or of a sash.

RUN — Small stream of paint.

SAG — A much wider stream of paint running down a surface.

SASH — Section of window that holds the glass (also the FRAME).

SCRAPER — A stiff-bladed tool used to scrape off flaking paint.

SIDING — Finish covering of the outside wall of a frame building.

SKINNING — Skin that forms over the surface of oil base paint.

SLEEVE — Cover that fits over roller handle; part that holds the paint.

SOFFIT — Underside of an overhanging cornice.

SPACKLE — A paste used to fill small cracks and holes.

SPACKLE KNIFE — Like a putty knife but has a flexible blade. Usually three or four inches wide.

STILE — Upright framing member in a panel door.

STIPPLE — Small dimples or dots in paint finish.

STRAIGHT EDGE — An edger used to get a clean line.

STRAIN — Remove dirt and lumps by means of pantyhose or wire screen.

STRIPPING — Removing paint or finish to get to bare wood.

STUCCO — Plaster used for exteriors made with Portland cement as its base.

SWEEP — A brush used for smoothing when hanging wallcovering.

THINNING — Adding thinner to paint (mineral spirits to oil, water to latex).

TIGHTEN — To fill in cracks between baseboard and wall.

TRIM — Finish materials in a building, such as moldings, baseboards, etc.

TRIMMING — Wallcovering selvage (trim), top or bottom.

TURPENTINE — Volatile oil used as a paint thinner.

UNDERCOATING — First coat to prepare surface for enamel finish; usually used in reference to interior painting.

VEHICLE — Liquid portion of paint consisting of binder (nonvolatile) and volatile thinners.

Paint Planner

Date: _____

Room _____

	Total SQ FT To Cover	Coverage Per Gal.	Gallons Needed	Cost Per Gal.	Total Cost For Room
CEILING First Coat					
Second Coat (if needed)					
WALLS First Coat					
Second Coat (if needed)					
TRIM First Coat			____ Qt. ☐ / ____ Gal. ☐		
Second Coat (if needed)			____ Qt. ☐ / ____ Gal. ☐		
Closet / Pantry First Coat			____ Qt. ☐ / ____ Gal. ☐		
Second Coat (if needed)			____ Qt. ☐ / ____ Gal. ☐		
Other					
Totals					

Room / Cost Estimator

Date:_____

Room _____

	Size of Room	Total SQ FT	Est. Gals. Needed	Cost Per Gal.	Sub Total
WALLS	length _____ ft. width _____ ft. height _____ ft. 2nd coat (if needed)	_____ sq.ft.	_____ Gal _____ Gal	$_____	$_____ $_____
CEILING	length _____ ft. width _____ ft. 2nd coat (if needed)	_____ sq.ft.	_____ Gal _____ Gal	$_____	$_____ $_____
TRIM	Windows _____ Doors _____ Baseboards _____ 2nd coat (if needed)		Qt. ☐ Gal. ☐ Qt. ☐ Gal. ☐	$_____	$_____ $_____
Closet / Pantry	Walls & Ceiling Door & Baseboard		_____ Qt. _____ Qt.	$_____	$_____ $_____
Floor	length _____ ft. width _____ ft.	_____ sq.ft.	_____ Gal	$_____	$_____
Totals for Room		_____ sq.ft.	_____ Gal	$ _____	

Room Painting History _____ (Room)

	Color Formula	Brand Name	Qty. Used	Cost	Who Painted	Date	Hours Spent
CEILING Undercoat			____ Gal.				
Finish Coat			____ Gal.				
WALLS Undercoat			____ Gal.				
Finish Coat			____ Gal.				
TRIM Undercoat			☐ Qt. ☐ Gal. ☐ Oil ☐ Latex				
Finish Coat			☐ Qt. ☐ Gal. ☐ Oil ☐ Latex				
CABINETS (Wood work) Undercoat			☐ Qt. ☐ Gal. ☐ Oil ☐ Latex				
Finish Coat			☐ Qt. ☐ Gal. ☐ Oil ☐ Latex				
Stain			☐ Qt. ☐ Gal. ☐ Varnish ☐ Polyurethane				
Closet / Pantry			☐ Qt. ☐ Gal.				
			Total	Total		Completed	Total
Other							
Comments							

Use This Tools and Equipment Checklist Before Starting Your Next Paint Job

Brushes

Bristle (for alkyd oil base paint)				Polyester / Nylon (for latex paint)			
Size	Qty.	Condition	Need To Get	Size	Qty.	Condition	Need To Get
1 1/2" or 2" Trim brush				1 1/2" or 2" Trim brush			
3" Doors Wide Trim				3" Doors Wide Trim			
4" Siding				4" Siding			

Tools & Equip	On Hand	Need To Get	Tools & Equip	On Hand	Need To Get
Interior			**General Tools**		
Drop cloth			Mineral Spirits/Turps		
Masking Tape			Pot Hooks		
Nail Set			Putty		
Roller(s)			Rubber Gloves		
Spackle			Sand Paper		
Spackle Knife			Scraper		
Steel Wool			Scrub Brush		
Tray			Stirrers		
Exterior			**Wall Covering**		
Buckets			Carpenter's Level		
Caulking			Plumb Bob		
Caulking Gun			Scissors		
Chisel Knife			Seam Roller		
Garden Hose			Size		
Safety Glasses			Smoother Brush		
Extension Ladder			Sponge		
Step Ladder			Razor Knife & Blades		
			Water Bucket		
			Wallpaper Table		
			Water Box		

Home Owners Inventory - Paint Supplies

Exterior Primer
Latex ☐
Alkyd ☐

Brand _____
Used for _____
Color / Tint _____
New (Unopened) ☐
Used When ? _____
How much left ?   Gal. _____ Qt. _____
Condition _____
Comments _____

Exterior Finish
Latex ☐
Alkyd ☐

Brand _____
Used for _____
Color / Tint _____
New (Unopened) ☐
Used When ? _____
How much left ?   Gal. _____ Qt. _____
Condition _____
Comments _____

Exterior Trim - Primer
Latex ☐
Alkyd ☐

Brand _____
Used for _____
Color / Tint _____
New (Unopened) ☐
Used When ? _____
How much left ?   Gal. _____ Qt. _____
Condition _____
Comments _____

Exterior Trim - Finish
Latex ☐
Alkyd ☐

Brand _____
Used for _____
Color / Tint _____
New (Unopened) ☐
Used When ? _____
How much left ?   Gal. _____ Qt. _____
Condition _____
Comments _____

Interior Undercoat
Wall ☐   Latex ☐
Ceiling ☐   Alkyd ☐

Brand _____
Used - room(s) _____
Color / Tint _____
New (Unopened) ☐
Used When ? _____
How much left ?   Gal. _____ Qt. _____
Condition _____
Comments _____

Interior Finish
Wall ☐   Latex ☐
Ceiling ☐   Alkyd ☐

Brand _____
Used room(s) _____
Color / Tint _____
New (Unopened) ☐
Used When ? _____
How much left ?   Gal. _____ Qt. _____
Condition _____
Comments _____

Interior Trim Undercoat
Latex ☐
Alkyd ☐

Brand _____
Used - room(s) _____
Color / Tint _____
New (Unopened) ☐
Used When ? _____
How much left ?   Gal. _____ Qt. _____
Condition _____
Comments _____

Interior Trim Finish
Latex ☐
Alkyd ☐

Brand _____
Used room(s) _____
Color / Tint _____
New (Unopened) ☐
Used When ? _____
How much left ?   Gal. _____ Qt. _____
Condition _____
Comments _____

Index

A

Acrylic emulsion size, 61, 62, 69
Acrylic paint, 13, 14, 20
Aluminum siding, 23-4, 32
American Single Roll, 68
Archways, curved, wallpapering, 75-6
Archways, rectangular, wallpapering, 75
Asbestos shingles, 33
Asphalt driveway, spilled paint on, 117
Asphalt shingles, 33

B

Backpriming, 120
Baseboards, 52-3
Bathroom, best paint for, 53
Blistering, 24
Blockwork, see Foundations
"Boxing" paint, 29-30, 101-2
Brass, cleaning, 39, 59
Brick, 32
Brushes, 108, 120
    care of, 99-101
    cleaning, 15, 99, 101, 123-4
    exterior, 27, 29
    latex, 99, 123-4
    latex, 99
    oil, 99-100
    oil paint, 123

Burning paint, 23
Buying paint, 19-20, 120-1

C

Cabinets, wallpapering around, 75
Ceiling paint, 19, 20
Ceilings, 15, 39, 59
    "cutting in", 44, 45, 59
    painting, 44, 47
    wallpapering, 75
    washing, 39, 47
Cement stain, 83
Chalking paint, 32, 34
Cleaning brushes, 15
Cleaning rollers, 118-9
Cleaning spilled paint, 117
Cleanup, 124
Clothing for painting, 118
Color of paint, 15
    selecting, 53
Cracks,
    filling, 39, 59
    scraping, 40
Crater, Warren H., 127
Creosote stain, 83
"Cutting in" ceilings, 44, 45, 59

D

Dampness, latex paint, 28
Deck paint, 31

Decking stain, 83
Doors, 32, 50-2
Double-hung windows, 47-8
Dropcloths, 26, 38, 58, 108
Drywall, 54
Dye lot, wallcovering, 69

E

Enamel finish, 18
Enamel undercoater, 18, 20, 47
Equipment, 107-112
Estimating, 89-97
Estimating time to complete job, 93-4
European Single Roll, 68
Extension ladder, 105-6, 107
Exterior and interior paints, differences, 19
Exterior finish coat, 29-35
    equipment, 29
Exterior paint, 13-15, 20
    applying, 24
    blistering, 24
    choosing, 14
    latex paint, 13-14, 20, 26, 34
        advantages, 14
        disadvantages, 14
    life, 23
    oil base, 13, 14, 26, 34
    peeling, 24

Exterior painting,
    equipment, 21
    weather, 27
Exterior preparation, 21-4
Exterior prime coat, 25-8
    equipment, 25
Exterior staining, 81-3
Exterior surfaces, 32-3
    aluminum siding, 32
    asbestos shingles, 33
    asphalt shingles, 33
    brick, 32
    stucco, 33
    wood shingles, 32-3

F

Fences, 83
Fingernail test, 18, 50, 55, 60
Finish, 20
    enamel, 18
    exterior, 23
    latex, 54
Finish coat, exterior, 29-35
Finish paint, 14
    oil base enamel, 18, 60
Flat latex, 13
Floors,
    applying finish, 87-8
    refinishing, 85-8
    refinishing, equipment, 85
    refinishing, shortcut version, 88
    removing stains, 87
    sanding, 85-7
Foundations, 31

G

Garage doors, 120
Glossary, 143
Grease, 39
Gutters and downspouts, 31, 120

H

High gloss latex, 13
Historic aspects of painting, 131-3
Home Owners Inventory — Paint
    Supplies, 115, 155

House, parts of, 92
Huck, Pat, 127, 129

I

Interior and exterior paints,
    differences, 19
Interior latex paint, advantages, 15,
    20
Interior paint, 15-20
    purchase guide, 19
Interior painting, 37-56
    equipment, 37
Interior staining, 79-80

K

Kitchen, best paint for, 53
Kitchen cabinets, 52

L

Label analysis, 103
Labels, 19-20
Ladder,
    extension, 105-6, 107
    parts, 104
    using, 27, 30-1
Latex,
    flat, 13
    high gloss, 13
    semi-gloss, 13
Latex brushes, 99, 123
Latex enamel semi-gloss, 19
Latex exterior paint,
    advantages, 14
    disadvantages, 14
Latex finish, 54
Latex interior paint, advantages,
    15, 20
Latex paint, exterior, 20, 26, 34
Latex primer, 19, 20
Latex undercoater, 19
Latex wall and ceiling finish, 19
Life of exterior paint, 23
Lining paper, 62
Linseed oil paint, 14
Liquid Masking Tape, 50

M

Masking tape, 121-2
Masonry conditioner, 33
Measuring a room, 37
Measuring a room for
    wallcovering, 67-8
Measuring house exterior, 25-6, 89-
    92
Measuring house interior, 93
Metric Single Roll, 68
Mildew removal, 21-2
Mistakes, 139-41

N

New room, 54-6

O

Oil base enamel finish paint, 18, 60
Oil base paint, 30
    exterior, 13, 14, 26, 34
Oil base primer, 20
Oil paint brushes, 99-100, 123
"One coat" paint, 19-20
One-coat painting, 33-5
Opening paint can, 16
Overpainting, 121
Oxalic acid, 87

P

Paint,
    burning, 23
    composition, 102
    exterior, choosing, 14
Paint Planner, 95, 147
Paint purchase guide, interior, 19
Paneled room, 53-4
Patching plaster, 39
Patterns of wallcovering, 76
Peeling, 24
Pigment, 13
Poly brush applicator, 50
Porches and steps, 31
Power roller, 109
Power washer, 109

Primer, 14, 15, 18, 20, 60, 122
    latex, 19, 20
    oil base, 20
    tinting, 26

Q

Questions about exterior painting, 23-4
Questions about interior painting, 53

R

Radiators, wallpapering around, 74-5
Removing wallpaper, 57-9
    equipment, 57
Removing wallpaper paste, 58
Repainting a room, 38-47
    preparation, 38-44
Roller tray, using, 17
Rollers, cleaning, 118-9
Roof, spilled paint on, 117
Room Painting History, 97, 151
Room/Cost Estimator, 96, 149
Rope, 108

S

Sander for scraping, 23
Sanding after first interior coat, 55
Satin finish paint, 18
Scrapers, 108
Scraping, using sander, 23
Scraping exterior paint, 22-3
Screens, removing paint, 119
"Self-covering" paint, 14
Semi-gloss,
    latex, 13
    latex enamel, 19
    paint, 18
Semi-transparent penetrating stain, 81-2
Shellac, 88
Shingles,
    asbestos, 33
    asphalt, 33
    wood, 32-3

Shrubs, trimming and covering, 26-7
Shutters, 32
    marking, 32
Size, acrylic emulsion, 61, 62, 69
Smoke stain, 39, 47
Soaking wallcovering, 76
Spackle, 39
Spilled paint, 117
Stain,
    applying and finishing, 80
    "boxing", 82
    cement, 83
    creosote, 83
    decking, 83
    getting the right shade, 80
    semi-transparent rating, 81-2
    solid, 82
    water-repellent preservative, 81
"Stain kill", 39
Staining, 79-84
    equipment, 79
    exterior, 81-3
    interior, 79-80
Staining floors, 80
Staining new trim, 79-80
Stepladder, 107
Stir sticks, 109
Stirring paint, 16
Storage life of paint, 118
Storage of paint, 105
Straight edge, 50
Straining paint, 52, 103, 59-60, 118
Stucco, 33

T

Temperature for painting, 23
Textured wallcovering, 76
Thinning paint, 27, 30
Time of year for painting, 23
Tools and Equipment Checklist, 113, 153
Tools for painting, 110
Touchup, 119-20
Trim paint, 18
Trim painting, 47, 50, 52-3

Trim, 30-2, 35, 38, 39, 59
    staining, 79-80
    washing, 39

U

Undercoater and wallcovering, 61-2
Undercoater, 18, 20, 47, 54, 122
    latex, 19

V

Vehicle, 13
Vinyl wallcovering, 62

W

Wall and ceiling finish, latex, 19
Wallcovering, 61-3
    dye lot, 69
    hanging, 65-77
        equipment, 65
        pre-pasted, 70-6
    lining, 62
    measuring, 70
        for window, 73-4
    nonpasted, 76-7
    overlapping, 74
    paper, 62
    patterns, 76
    pitfalls, 61-2
    pre-pasted vinyl, 61
    preparing walls, 68-70
    removing, 69
    soaking, 76
    textured, 76
    tips, 76
    tools, 66
    types, 62-3, 68
        adhesives, 68
    types of rolls, 68
    vinyl, 62
Wallpaper,
    removing, 57-9
        equipment, 57
    soaking, 58
Wallpaper paste, removing, 58

Wallpapering,
    adjusting corners, 74
    around cabinets, 75
    around obstacles, 74-6
    around radiators, 74-5
    ceilings, 75
    curved archways, 75-6
    new walls, 69
    over old wallpaper, 62, 69
    previously painted walls, 69
    rectangular archways, 75

Walls, 15, 39
    washing, 39
Washing woodwork, 39
Water base paint, *see Latex*
Water stain, 47
Water-repellent preservative, 81
Weather and exterior painting, 27
Weather and paint, 118
When to paint, 121
Window, measuring for
    wallcovering, 73-4

Window glass, replacing, 124-5
Windows,
    double-hung, 47
    exterior, 30
    interior, 47-50
Wood preservative, 33
Wood shingles, 32-3
Woodwork, 54-5
    lumps and sags, 52-3
    washing, 39